SPIRITUAL STARS AND WEALTH STARS

A Practical Guide for Your Home and Office

SPIRITUAL STARS AND WEALTH STARS

A Practical Guide for Your Home and Office

Master Feng Shui Researcher

Rikako Fujiki

Spiritual Stars and Wealth Stars:
A Practical Guide for Your Home and Office

ISBN: 978-1-64273-428-7

Project Editor: Yumi Itabashi, Hachidori Inc.
Editor: Andrew Kirkham

Printed in Japan
1 2 3 4 5 6 7 8 9 10

43-32 22nd Street STE 204 Long Island City New York 11101
www.onepeacebooks.com

Table of contents

Foreword

An Encounter with Feng Shui and Spiritualism

I first encountered the "Law" of William James (American psychologist and philosopher) via the Japanese journalist and non-fiction writer Takashi Tachibana's book, "Near-Death Experience." That law was described as follows: "it looks as if the 'spirits' have been ordered to provide just enough evidence to convince those who are willing to be convinced, but never enough to win over the sceptics."[1] Put the same phenomenon before two people, and the one who does not want to believe will claim that there is sufficient doubt to deny it, and the one who does want to believe, that there is sufficient evidence to believe.

I am the type that wants to believe, and the first time I became aware of the existence of a world I could not see was when I was 20 years old and my pet cat passed away. After days of not being able to think straight, one day, I suddenly had the image of my cat existing somewhere before being born and coming to me upon entering this world, and that they had only returned to the place from which they came. Let alone sufficient evidence, I didn't have any basis for this at all, and yet I felt certain of it. That day was the turning point for me moving past the grief of losing my pet, but ever since, I have been a voracious reader of books on the afterlife and on the world we cannot see. Among them, there was a series of books known as the "Silver Birch Series."

This series is a collection of stories and sayings delivered by an ancient spirit known as "Silver Birch." Maurice Barbanell, the editor of an English spiritualism magazine, was the medium for the spirit. The collection emerged from seances that began in the 1920s and lasted for nearly 50 years, at a pace of one meeting a week. In these seances, Silver Birch was not present as a human body, but as a spirit.[2] After death, humans leave behind their physical body and enter a spirit life.[3] It is said that when we are asleep, our souls travel to the spirit realm, where they can encounter other souls and experience the world after death. There is endless discussion over what gods are, what the difference is between this world and the one beyond, why humans exist, what the purpose of our lives is, etc. If the type of person who does not want to believe were to read about such supernatural phenomena, they may only see it as fantasy, as idle talk, or even irresponsible.

The term "supernatural phenomenon" has different connotations, but Feng Shui is also a field that involves interacting with a world that modern science is unable to explain. Why does placing a pendulum clock or an indoor fountain in a particular place bring fortune? This is not something that modern science would be able to answer even if it tried. This is a world closed to those who do not want to believe.

As the type of person who wants to believe in strange things that science cannot explain, I quickly became a devotee of feng shui during the feng shui boom that took place in Japan nearly 30 years ago. I cleared out unneeded things, applied myself to cleaning up, placed crystals and zodiac ornaments in my bedroom and foyer, just as I was told.

However, at some point, I stopped engaging in these "feng shui strategies." Maybe it was because I wasn't feeling any definite effects from them. As I was unable to acquire "enough evidence to believe," at some point I ended up filing feng shui away as "something I don't believe."

Nonetheless, some time later I encountered Flying Star Feng Shui, which pulled feng shui out of the "don't believe" file and returned it to the "believe" file. That's how impressed I was by its accuracy. This school of feng shui was able to provide explanations not only for my immediate family, but for the history of my grandparents, my friends, and my acquaintances, all in a general framework. Soon after I began my study of Flying Star Feng Shui, I spent 6 years living in Singapore, a city with a deep connection to this school of feng shui. This experience only served to make my belief in it stronger. Unlike the feng shui of my earlier failed attempt, this feng shui was based on an orderly theory, replete with tangible, definitive evidence. It may have been the first time that I saw such clear evidence used to describe the "world that science can't explain."

Flying Star Feng Shui is an ancient form of astronomy discovered by the sages of ancient China. Just like Western astrology, which originated in ancient Babylon, its source of information was the starry sky. Just as the term "flying star" suggests, the process involves deciphering how the energy expressed by the stars is distributed through architecture, which stars provide what kinds of energy, and methods to harness that energy. From there, the basic idea is to improve people's fortune, health, and personal relationships through the employment of suitable techniques. In technical terms, the star that governs fortune is called the Water Star and the star that governs health and relationships is called the Mountain Star. If the auspicious Water Star is present in the foyer, living room, staircase, or atrium, that house will be blessed with good fortune. If the auspicious Mountain Star is present in the bedroom, study, or an executive office, health and relationships are expected to improve. However, why is it that the auspicious Mountain Star is best-suited to rush through a bedroom or study? Why would the auspicious Mountain Star being in an executive office help smooth over internal business relationships?

In modern science, there are various means of recording brain activity, including a way to replicate images conjured up in the brain on a computer screen.

In such experiments, it has apparently been found that [4] *"while humans continue dreaming up until the moment they awake, they forget everything except for the final 30 seconds"* According to the previously mentioned Silver Birch, humans experience the world after death while asleep: perhaps there is some relationship between this and the dreams we cannot recall. Perhaps those things that we forget at the level of memory were involved in communication with something at a deeper level.

If, as Silver Birch claimed, humans enter the spirit realm while they are asleep, perhaps having the auspicious Mountain Star flying through the bedroom enables one to make a deep connection to that realm while sleeping and obtain good advice. Even when not sleeping, having the auspicious Mountain Star rushing through the study may result in wonderful inspirations while writing. Managers are always faced with decisions that they must make as they run their businesses. If the auspicious Mountain Star is rushing through an executive office, perhaps they can receive inspiration that improves their performance and raises company morale. Recently, the number of people incorporating meditation into their daily lives is increasing all over the world. The place they choose to meditate may be a good place to let the auspicious Mountain Star fly through. Perhaps, areas with the auspicious Mountain Star can be associated with the root of inspiration found in tranquil environments.

In order to make this book more accessible to readers who are unfamiliar with feng shui terminology, the Water Star is referred to as the Wealth Star and the Mountain Star is referred to as the Spiritual Star. Furthermore, while Flying Star charts are traditionally read with south as "up," the charts in this book have been adjusted so that they can be read like most maps, with north as "up."

In countries like Taiwan and Singapore that are the home of Flying Star Feng Shui, experienced feng shui consultants are available, but even if you can't find one, you can actually ask just about anyone for advice. That said, in order to assess your home or office using Flying Star Feng Shui, you'll need a luopan *(geomantic compass)* as well as a basic understanding of yin and yang theory, the Five Elements, and 8 Trigrams. All of this could be a little intimidating for someone who wants to give feng shui techniques a try—I think that's a shame.

In order to communicate the wonders of Flying Star Feng Shui, even if only to one more person, this book has had all difficult language and theory removed, providing simple explanations on how to create a personal Flying Star chart for your home or office and how to use it. Once you've made your Flying Star chart, which maps out the energy of your building, the rest is easy. The things you'll need are all little things that you likely have lying around. You don't have to worry about your house taking on an obvious Chinese decor style.

For those who want to know more about this school of feng shui, the final chapter contains a discussion of the basics of the ancient Chinese science from which it emerged.

Flying Star Feng Shui is a pragmatic environmental science meant to provide, as much as possible, the inspiration you need to acquire the money we need to survive and the health and social vibrance we need to thrive. As the proverb goes, "God helps those who help themselves." Why not try "helping yourself" to the improvements in your environment that feng shui offers?

I believe that this school of feng shui is a revelation: a divine revelation, received in deep sleep by the sages of ancient China, after long contemplation of the starry sky and the invaluable wisdom it contains.

---

1) In a moment of exasperation, William James suggested another explanation for the vagaries of the 'spirits': I confess that at times I have been tempted to believe that the Creator has eternally intended this department of nature to remain baffling, to prompt our curiosities and hopes and suspicions all in equal measure, so that, although ghosts and clairvoyances and raps and messages from spirits ... can never be fully explained away, they can also never be susceptible of full corroboration. Or, to put it another way, it looks as if the 'spirits' have been ordered to provide just enough evidence to convince those who are willing to be convinced, but never enough to win over the sceptics. This notion—which we might call James's Law—must have crossed the mind of everybody who has taken an interest in the paranormal. The evidence is abundant and plentiful, but it always leaves room for doubt.
p.158-159 Wilson, Colin. Afterlife. Knopf Doubleday Publishing Group. Kindle edition.

2) Guidance from Silver Birch Edited by Anne Dooley
P.19 Chapter 2 Who are you?
Who are you? Do you know? You know just that faces that is expressed through your body, but that is only the pin point as distinct from the larger life which is beyond it. You must get the proper perspective. You must realize that the spirit is the supreme part of you. The spirit is the higher, the body is the lower. The spirit is the aster, the body is the servant.

3) Light from Silver Birch Edited by Pam Riva
P.56 Chapter 6 What will happen when you die?
Actually, every one of you travels astral when you go to sleep. Then your spirit, for the time being, departs from your body, roams into our world and meets souls you love and who love you. It is a divine provision by which preparation is made for the time when you come here, so that it will not be a shock. When you do come you will remember, and be ready for the many wonderful happenings that spirit life that spirit life has to offer you. It could be said that you die every night.

4) Ginga no Katasumide Kagakuyawa by Zen Takujyu
P.114 The Ethics of Forgotten Dreams

Chapter 1

Flying Star Feng Shui: The Astronomy of Ancient China

The reason why Flying Star feng shui is now found mostly in Taiwan, Hong Kong, and Singapore

The beginnings of Flying Star Feng Shui reach back as far as 2,637 BC.[1] The oldest record is thought to be the nine stars recorded in colors and numbers on the almanac painted on the walls of the caves at Tun Huang (Dunhuang), during the Tang dynasty (618–907AD).[2]

The Tang dynasty was the period in which large numbers of scholars from foreign countries were studying in China. It is said that Emperor Xuanzong forbade the transmission of feng shui techniques to any of these foreign scholars from Japan, Korea, and Mongolia.[3]

As dynasties rose and fell, Flying Star feng shui techniques remained hidden from the general public, and it is presumed that they were passed down as an oral tradition by feng shui practitioners under strict secrecy. While Flying Star feng shui was a top state secret during the Tang dynasty, it was eventually revealed to the public with the fall of the Qing dynasty in 1912, by the feng shui practitioner, Master Sam Chuk Yin.

Master Sam Chuk Yin [4]

At the end of the Qing dynasty, a certain feng shui lover who had received a Western education immersed themselves in an experimental study of this ancient Chinese science that had been veiled in secrecy for so long.

Master Sam Chuk Yin was born in Hangzhou two years before the Taiping Rebellion (1851–1864).

He was captured when he was 13, when the Taiping army occupied Hangzhou; later, in Shanghai, he encountered an opportunity to receive a Western education in English. He was employed by Captain Charles Gordon to translate Western strategy and tactics books and assisted in training the Chinese military. He was interested in feng shui from a young age, and studied traditional feng shui in order to find a suitable graveyard for his father – but he found that it was rife with defects. One day, he found a book on feng shui on a bookshelf at the home of one of his friends. That book was on Flying Star Feng Shui, and it addressed all

---

1) *Pg.18, 48 "Feng Shui Essentials" by Raymond Lo, Feng Shui Lo*
2) *Pg.62 "Feng Shui History" by Stephen Skinner, Golden Hoard Press Pte Ltd*
3) *Pg.9 'Feng Shui Essentials" by Raymond Lo, Feng Shui Lo*
4) *Pg.11 "Feng Shui Essentials" by Raymond Lo, Feng Shui Lo*
Pg.117–122 "Feng Shui History" by Stephen Skinner, Golden Hoard Press Pte Ltd

his prior concerns. Beginning with this book, he threw himself into researching this school of feng shui. Upon his passing, his eldest son compiled the fruit of this research and published it as a book titled "Master Sam's Xuan Kong." Today, it remains the bible of Flying Star Feng Shui throughout the world. The first edition was published in 1925, with an expanded edition published in 1933. While there are now several subschools of Flying Star Feng Shui, the feng shui described in this book is based on the theories described in Master Sam's Xuan Kong.

The Fall of the Qing Dynasty

The other event that brought Flying Star feng shui to the hands of the people was the fall of the Qing dynasty in 1912. Until this point, feng shui practitioners were hidden away by the imperial family and the high officials for whom they worked, and they now had no choice but to open their doors to everyday business and citizens. After the founding of the People's Republic of China, the "eradication of superstition campaigns" carried out by the Chinese Community Party resulted in a diaspora of oppressed feng shui practitioners to Taiwan, Hong Kong, and parts of Malaysia, including Singapore. As a result of this emigration, Flying Star Feng Shui lived on. The small number of experts in Chinese metaphysics that remained ended up being forced to emigrate to the West at the time of the Cultural Revolution. In their view, they had been shut off from the Chinese-speaking world, so little by little, they began to introduce Flying Star Feng Shui, in all its ancient and novel variety, to the societies of the West.

What is Feng Shui?

Feng shui is a collaboration between visible and invisible energy in the environment. It is, in simple terms, a suite of techniques for avoiding calamity and maximizing one's natural luck by rearranging one's surroundings. In the case of economic fortune, for example, people are born with some amount of luck in this regard, but feng shui can enable that luck to reach its maximum potential through manipulation of one's environment.

There are two types of environments. One is the environment we can see: the land, the shape of a room, colors, aspects of interior design such as furniture and windows (and the outside scenery they reveal), as well as roads, etc. The other is invisible force. You can think of the directionality that is revealed by a magnetic compass as an example.

Feng shui techniques utilize the interaction between visible things and invisible energies in a building in order to maximize the health and fortune of people living in it.

The Emergence of Flying Star Feng Shui

The ancient Chinese, in their observations of the night sky, came to the conclusion that "time" also belongs to the realm of invisible energy. The passage of time can result in the energy of a building becoming inauspicious or changing its quality. In other words, they discovered that **the passage of time leads to changes in energy.** This is one of the defining traits of Flying Star Feng Shui that separates it from other forms of feng shui.

A once-flourishing business that, one year, suddenly goes into decline and disappears before you know it, may be an example of the sort of case that can be explained with Flying Star Feng Shui.

The Nine Stars of the Big Dipper

Flying Star Feng Shui is a school of feng shui that describes how to strengthen economic fortune and health by understanding how nine stars (energies) are distributed throughout a building and manipulating them in order to strengthen the auspicious stars and diminish the inauspicious stars. **It makes it possible to identify the power spots of a building as they were first discovered by the sages of ancient China.**

It is said that these nine stars are derived from the stars in the Big Dipper. While the Big Dipper is formally defined by seven stars, these nine stars are all focused around Polaris, the North Star, revolving around it at a pace of one revolution per year. By determining how these stars move, or fly, through a building, the economic fortune and luck in health of that building can be determined. All nine stars have their own names, but in Flying Star Feng Shui, they are simply referred to by number, from 1 to 9.

Each flying star holds two types of energy. One of these types governs economic fortune, and is called the Wealth Star. The other governs health and human relationships, and is called the Spiritual Star.

The techniques of Flying Star Feng Shui divide a floor plan into nine areas: the cardinal directions of north, south, east west, northeast, northwest, southwest, and southeast, and the center. The flying star of each of these areas is then appraised.

Each of the nine bearings has both a Wealth Star and Spiritual Star. Altogether, there are 18 stars spread out to the nine bearings, with two stars per bearing.

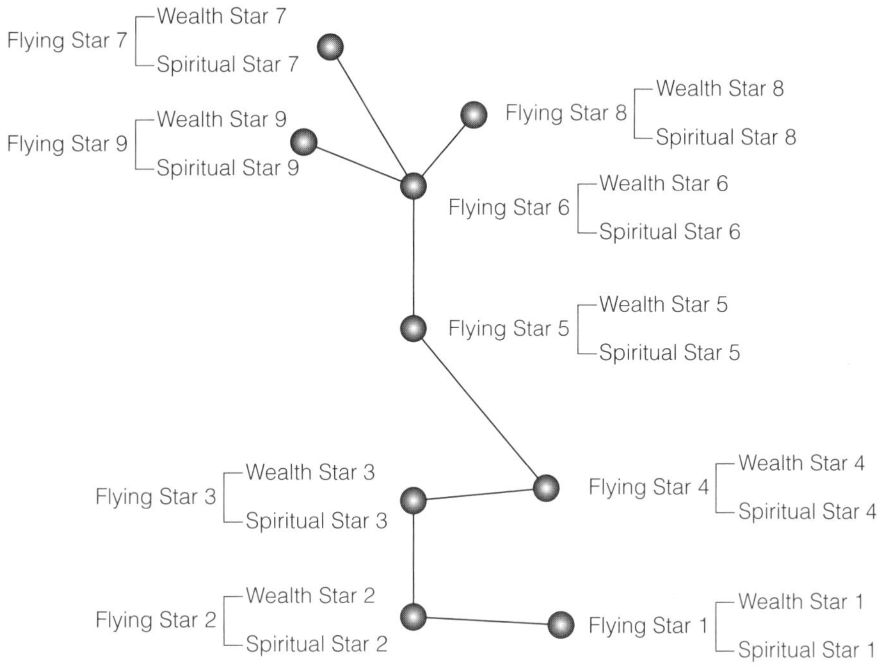

Stylized by author with reference to original: Pg.23 "Feng Shui Essentials" by Raymond Lo, Feng Shui Lo

Figure 1: The Nine Stars of the Big Dipper

The two stars do not express their respective energies at the same time. Based on how a particular bearing is used, one of the stars will express its energy. Using the living space in the figure below as an example, the bedroom in the southern bearing has Wealth Star 6 and Spiritual Star 9, but when using it as a bedroom, Spiritual Star 9 will express its energy. The entrance in the eastern bearing has Wealth Star 9 and Spiritual Star 3, but because it›s an entrance, Wealth Star 9 will express its energy.

Places where the Wealth Star expresses energy

Entrance, living room, dining room, kitchen

Staircase, atrium, elevator, escalator

Places where the Spiritual Star expresses energy

Bedroom, study, executive office

Whether or not a store or company flourishes and whether or not a household will be prosperous is based on where the auspicious Wealth Star flies and what kind of environment it is in. The health and relationships of residents of a building, similarly are guided by how the auspicious Spiritual Star flies through it, what sorts of environments it is in. This energy map is called a Flying Star chart. It can be seen as an energy map of the power spots of a building as discovered and described by the sages of ancient China. Once a flying star chart is complete, next the rooms are divided in accordance with their bearing, and their respective flying stars are filled in to accord with the chart (Figure 3).

Flying Star chart

Figure 2 is the Flying Star chart of the apartment.

For the numbers in each bearing, the number on the left is the Spiritual Star, and the number on the right is the Wealth Star.

For example, the north bearing contains Spiritual Star 1 and Wealth Star 7. Image A shows the Wealth Star and Spiritual Star for each bearing and which star will express its energy based on use.

[NOTE]

— *As mentioned above, traditional flying star charts are oriented with south as "up" and north as "down," but in this book, like regular maps, north is depicted as "up" and south is depicted as "down"*

— *The flying star for each bearing is determined by referring to the flying star chart.*

Figure 2: Flying Star Chart of Apartment

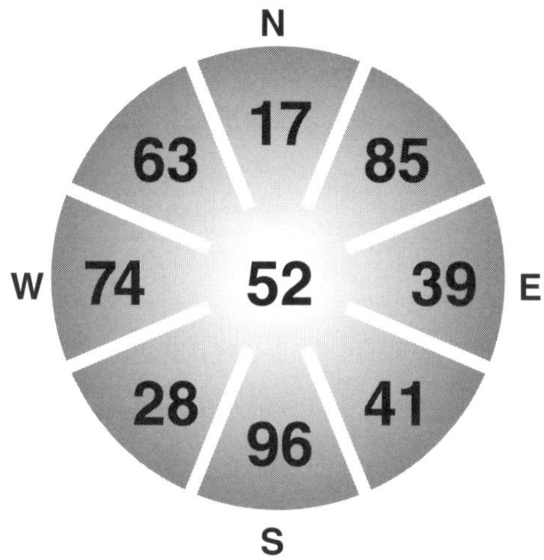

Figure 3: Floorplan showing the Wealth Star and Spiritual Star of each bearing according to the flying star chart

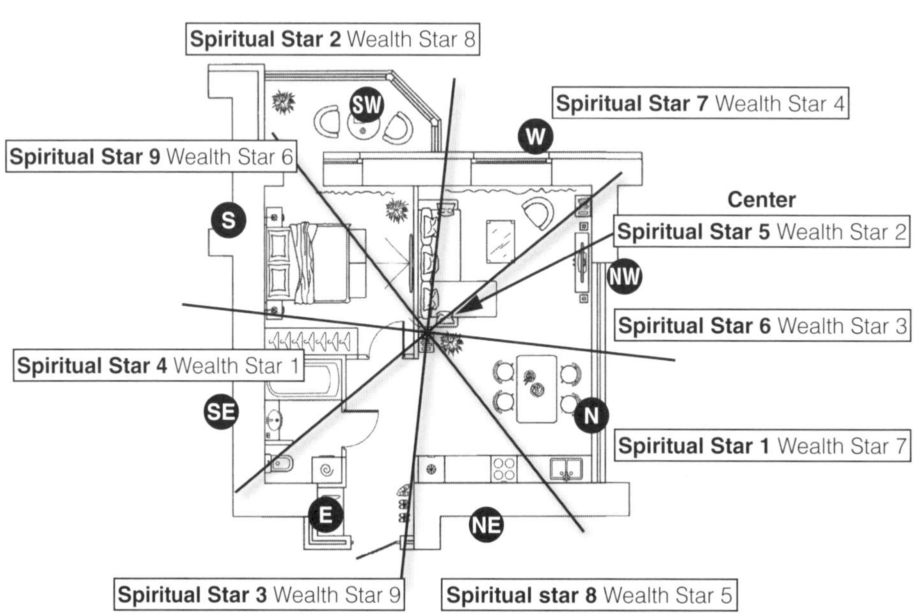

In this apartment, with the exception of the bedroom, Wealth Stars are expressing energy everywhere.

If the living room does not contain a TV, but rather is used as a study with a desk, Spiritual Stars will express energy in the north and northwest bearing.

Information needed to draw a flying star chart

To draw a flying star chart, the following is necessary.

— The year in which people occupied the building after its construction
A building completed construction in 2023(Age of 8), but left empty until 2024, is considered as Age of 9 building.
— The direction towards which the building faces

As mentioned previously, the major difference between Flying Star Feng Shui and other forms of feng shui is its consideration of the passage of time. The flying star chart, as an energy map of a building, is informed by the bearing towards which the building faces and its year of completed construction (the year in which people became active in it).

Every 20 years makes a unit, which is referred to as an Age.

Age 9 1844–1863

Age 1 1864–1883
Age 2 1884–1903
Age 3 1904–1923
Age 4 1924–1943
Age 5 1944–1963
Age 6 1964–1983
Age 7 1984–2003
Age 8 2004–2023
Age 9 2024–2043

Age 1 2044–2063

[NOTE]

These years do not begin on January 1st like years in the Western calendar. In ancient Chinese science, a new year begins on Lichun on February 3rd (or 4th) until the day before Lichun of the following year. Age 8, therefore, lasts until the day before Lichun in 2024, and Age 9 begins with Lichun in 2024 (February 4th).*

In the ancient Chinese calendar, one year is split into 24 seasons based on the movement of the sun.

**Lichun is the first day of spring, which is regarded as the start of a new year.*

After Lichun in 2044, there will be a return to Age 1. These 180 years (20 years times 9 Ages) demarcate the frequency at which all of the planets in the Solar System align, while the 20-year period of an Age is drawn from the frequency at which Jupiter and Saturn align.

This 20-year method of dividing time began in 2,637 BC, and continues to this day

For example, the interior energy map for a building that finished construction and had people begin to live in 2020 would use the Age 8 flying star chart. Whether or not the Age advances to Age 9, or Age 1, the chart for this building will not change until it is demolished.

—

The method for determining which bearing a building faces and its flying star chart and the means for applying the flying star chart to a floorplan are described in Chapter 3.

Chapter 2

The Wealth Star and The Spiritual Star

The Wealth Star

The Wealth Star brings fortune to the residents of a given building, but that doesn't mean all Wealth Stars will make people rich. Depending on the Age in question, only three of the nine Wealth Stars will bring economic fortune. Moreover, not all of them are equal in strength. In Age 8, which runs from 2004 to 2023, the Wealth Stars with the greatest energy are, in order, Wealth Star 8, Wealth Star 9, and Wealth Star 1. In Age 7, which runs from 1984 to 2003, the order is Wealth Star 7, Wealth Star 8, and Wealth Star 9.

This applies no matter what Age in which a building was constructed. For buildings constructed in Age 7, from 2004 to 2023 in Age 8, its strongest Wealth Star is Wealth Star 8. Therefore, an entrance through which Wealth Star 7 flies will be blessed with economic fortune in Age 7, but in Age 8, Wealth Star 7 becomes inauspicious, and no longer provides such fortune.

Strictly speaking, Age 8 lasts until the day before Lichun in 2024, but in this book, we'll assume that the energies of Age 9 have strengthened enough that it has already started by that point.

In Age 9, which begins in 2024, the strongest Wealth Stars and Spiritual Stars are Wealth Star 9 and Spiritual 9, followed by Wealth Star 1 and Spiritual Star 1. Unfortunately, Wealth Star 2 and Spiritual Star 2 are not considered the third set of auspicious stars in this case. Flying star 2 and flying star 5 are the strongest of the nine stars in yin energy, so while they are considered to lessen bad luck somewhat, they are not considered auspicious stars when they are third in the order.

Regardless of the Age, every flying star besides the auspicious stars has a particular nature, which together bring a variety of undesirable energies. Chapter 4 discusses these various effects, as well as methods for dealing with the negative energy.

Requirements for the Auspicious Wealth Star to Bring Financial Fortune

The most auspicious Wealth Star in the 20-year period beginning in 2024 is Wealth Star 9, but its mere existence is not enough for it to demonstrate its strength.

When the Wealth Star moves through entryway doors, open areas, windows facing roads and open areas, staircases, elevators, escalators, atriums, etc.–basically, any place with activity and movement–it will exert its effect. Whenever the above areas have an auspicious Wealth Star, that building will be blessed with financial fortune.

If Wealth Star 9 is not in any areas like those listed above, its activity can be enhanced with the placement of an indoor fountain or a pendulum clock.

Homes and Buildings Resistant to Financial Fortune

(1) Those for which the most auspicious Wealth Star is in the center bearing.

Until 2043, a Wealth Star 9 in the center bearing is unable to fly freely and thus is unable to bring financial fortune as the most auspicious Wealth Star. However, if there is a skylight in the center bearing, or a staircase or atrium, the Wealth Star is able to move actively and bring financial fortune.

(2) Those for which the most auspicious Wealth Star is in a bearing that the building does not cover, and is filled in by an adjacent building.

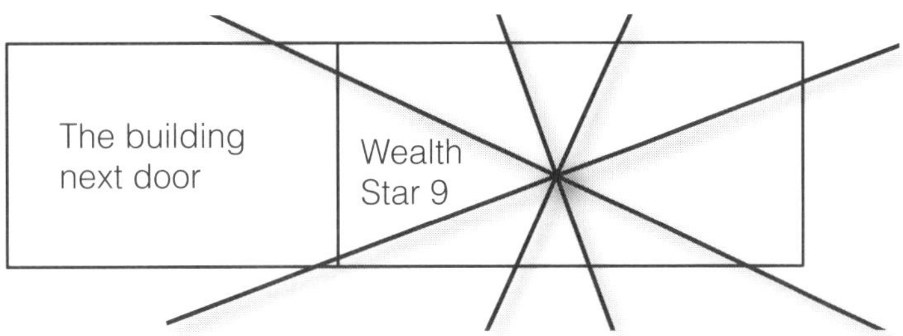

Figure 4: A Building that Resists Financial Fortune in Age 9

(3) A staircase or atrium in the center bearing with an inauspicious Wealth Star.

A staircase or atrium with an auspicious Wealth Star flying through it will enhance financial fortunes, but note that if the Wealth Star is inauspicious, it will have the opposite effect (see Chapter 4 for the effects of each inauspicious Wealth Star and their countermeasures)

(4) An entrance with an inauspicious Wealth Star.

In this case as well, see Chapter 4 for countermeasures.

Auspicious Spiritual Star

In contrast with the Wealth Star, which provides financial fortunes when in open, active environments, the Spiritual Star expresses an energy that affects health and human relationships when in quiet, closed spaces. Like Wealth Star 9, Spiritual Star 9 will be the most auspicious until 2043, followed by Spiritual Star 1. Like Wealth Star 2, Spiritual Star 2 should reduce bad luck, but not to the point of being an auspicious star.

At home

It is thought that sleeping in a room with an auspicious Spiritual Star will result in sound sleep. If one's entire body is not within the bearing of the auspicious Spiritual Star, the same effect can be obtained so long as one's head enters the area of that bearing. Even if a bedroom has an auspicious Spiritual Star, if it faces a pool, ocean, or busy street, the effect is lessened. This energy is best brought out when the room has small windows and is surrounded by tall buildings or trees. It is ideal if upon waking, an auspicious Wealth Star (Wealth Star 9 or Wealth Star 1 in Age 9) lies within 180 degrees of the direction one faces.

Store

Place the register in an area with an auspicious Spiritual Star. Ideally, an auspicious Wealth Star (Wealth Star 9 or Wealth Star 1 in Age 9) will be present in the 180 degree space in front of it.

Office

In an office, it is appropriate to select a bearing with an auspicious Spiritual Star for an executive office or desk. If a desk or room of someone without that status contains an auspicious Spiritual Star, it may cause issues for relationships in the office.

Ideally, an auspicious Wealth Star (Wealth Star 9 or Wealth Star 1 in Age 9) will be present in the 180 degree space in front of such a desk or office.

Altar

Similar to register placement, place in a bearing with an auspicious Spiritual Star facing a bearing with an auspicious Wealth Star within 180 degrees (Wealth Star 9 or Wealth Star 1 in Age 9). Place altars against a wall (never against a window).

Auspicious Spiritual Stars in Entrances, Staircases, and Atriums

Auspicious Spiritual Stars exhibit their effects best in quiet environments with little activity, so when they are in entrances, staircases, and atriums, it can have an undesirable effect on the health and relationships of the building's residents. In Age 9, homes with Spiritual Star 9 in their entryway should take caution. There is no particular way to deal with this problem. In this case, it is preferable to use a room with Spiritual Star 1 as a bedroom.

Kua Number: A Method for Choosing Bedrooms

In Age 9, the only auspicious stars for a bedroom are Spiritual Star 9 and Spiritual Star 1. In the event that the bearings in which these Spiritual Stars fly cannot be used for bedrooms, the Kua number offers a method for solving the problem of how to choose at least slightly preferable bedrooms for everyone.

What is a Kua Number?

Flying Star Feng Shui defines years not from January 1st to December 31st, but from Lichun (around February 3) to the day before Lichun of the following year. For each year, a chart can be made that shows which bearing the nine stars are flying towards. The number that appears in the center of that chart is the lifelong Kua number for boys born in that year. For example, the number at the center of the chart for 2023 is 4. For every boy born between Lichun in 2023 to the day before Lichun in 2024, their Kua number is 4. Even if they are born in the same year, the Kua number differs for males and females.

This number holds an important role in Flying Star Feng Shui when considering the flying stars of bedrooms and entrances.

How to Determine Kua Number (for Individuals Born Before 2000)

Male: Kua number is the remainder of (100–last two digits of Western birth year) ÷ 9

Female: Kua number is the remainder of (last two digits of Western birth year–4) ÷9

In case of no remainder, the Kua number is 9

How to Determine Kua Number (for Individuals Born After 2000)

Male: Kua number is equal to 11 – (sum of the digits in Western birth year)

Female: Kua number is equal to 4 + (sum of the digits in Western birth year)

If the number is larger than 9, subtract 9 to obtain the Kua number.

* If the Kua number is 5, the number changes as follows:

Male: Kua number = 2

Female: Kua number = 8

Spiritual Stars to Avoid in Bedrooms

It is not desirable for one's health for their bedroom to have the same Spiritual Star as their Kua number. For example, someone with Kua number 4 should avoid bedrooms with Spiritual Star 4. However, in Age 9, anyone can use Spiritual Stars 9 and 1. For those who have Kua numbers of 9 or 1, using Spiritual Stars 9 and 1 is no problem.

Based on the laws of the 5 elements, there are certain Spiritual Stars that should be avoided based on Kua number. The figure below shows the Spiritual Stars best avoided for each Kua number.

Kua number	Spiritual Stars to Avoid in Bedrooms
1	Spiritual Stars 2, 5, 8
2	Spiritual Stars 2, 5, 3, 4
3	Spiritual Stars 2, 5, 3, 6, 7
4	Spiritual Stars 2, 5, 4, 6, 7
6	Spiritual Stars 2, 5, 6 Spiritual Star 9 (except during Age 9)
7	Spiritual Stars 2, 5, 7 Spiritual Star 9 (except during Age 9)
8	Spiritual Stars 2, 5, 3, 4, 8
9	Spiritual Stars 2, 5, 9 (except during Age 9) Spiritual Star1(except during Ages 9 and 1)

Figure 5: Spiritual Stars to Avoid in Bedrooms

[NOTE] Reference 2 in Chapter 8 discusses the theory behind Spiritual Stars to avoid

Bed and desk placement

While feng shui describes techniques for improving people's health and fortune by using the interaction between visible and invisible energies, Flying Star Feng Shui focuses on the latter sort of energy.

What follows is a description of how to place beds in bedrooms and desks in offices, which are both visible forms of energy.

Ideal bed placement

— Place the bedrest against a wall.

— Place such that the door is on a diagonal line or is within line of sight.

[NOTE]

Avoid placing a mirror in a place where you can see yourself sleeping. If you are unable to move your mirror, place a cloth over it at night so that you aren't reflected.

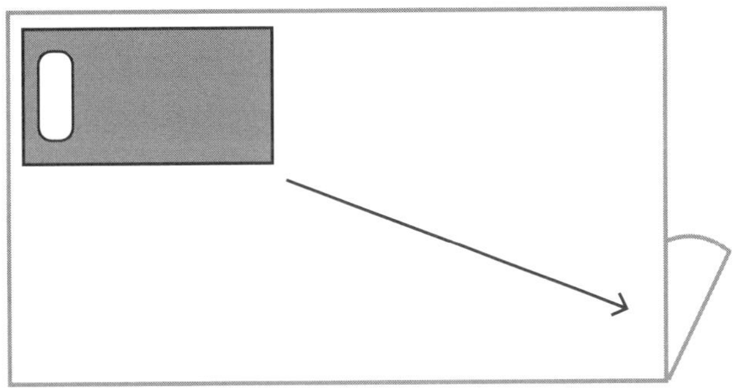

Ideal desk placement

— Place one edge against a wall

— Ensure your back will be against a wall

— Ensure the door is on a diagonal line from the desk (within your line of sight)

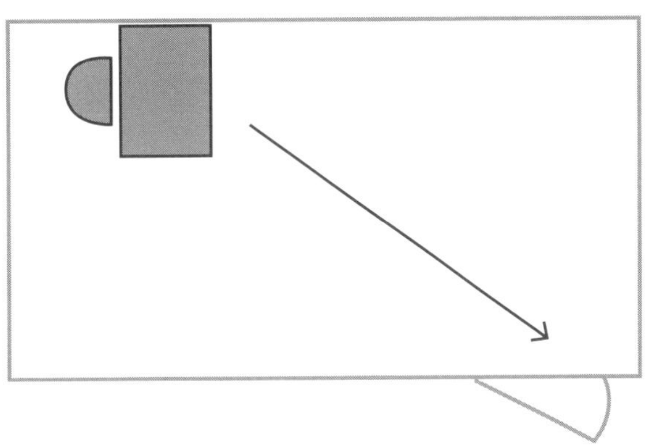

Should Spiritual Stars or Ideal Placements Receive Priority?

Sometimes the ideal placement of a bed or desk is in a location that is not ideal in terms of Spiritual Stars. Determining whether to prioritize visible or invisible energy is a difficult matter. If placing a bed in a location that seems comfortable results in a conflict with a Spiritual Star, I recommend keeping the bed there and taking countermeasures against the Spiritual Star (See Chapter 4).

Chapter 3

How to evaluate our personal space by Flying Star Feng Shui

In order to evaluate our personal space like home, office, shop etc. by Flying Star Feng Shui, we must fashion our Flying Star chart, which acts as an energy map superimposed on a floorplan.

How to establish a Flying Star chart

What follows is the method for establishing a Flying Star chart that describes where and how stars fly through a building.

1. Identify the Building's Age.

This is done by determining the year in which people first started using the building after construction was completed and comparing it to a chart of Ages (see Chapter 1)

Age 6: 1964–1983

Age 7: 1984–2003

Age 8: 2004–2023

Age 9: 2024–2043

2. Identify the Central Point of the Floorplan.

— How to identify the central point

Draw two diagonal lines through the plan. The intersection is the central point.

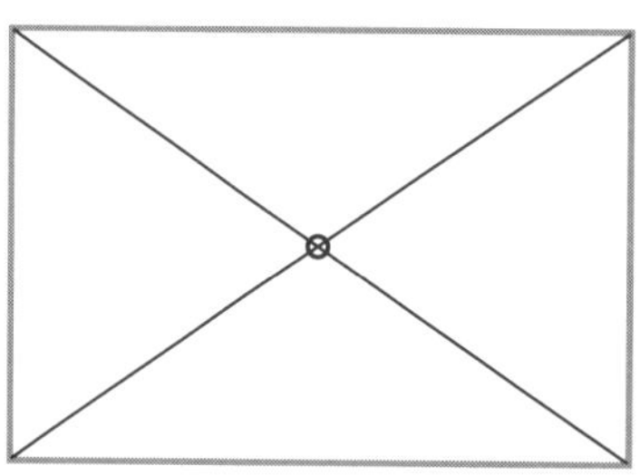

In cases where there is a recess in the building that is less than 1/2 the total length of each side it occupies, draw your diagonal lines as though the recess was not there.

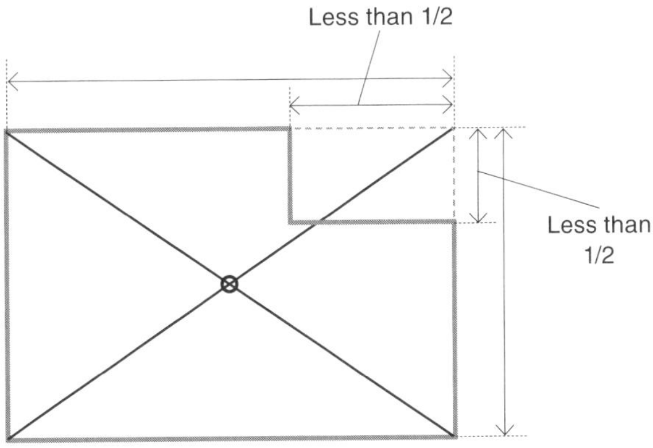

In cases where there is a protruding part of the building that is less than 1/2 the total length of each side it occupies, ignore the protrusion and treat the building as a rectangle.

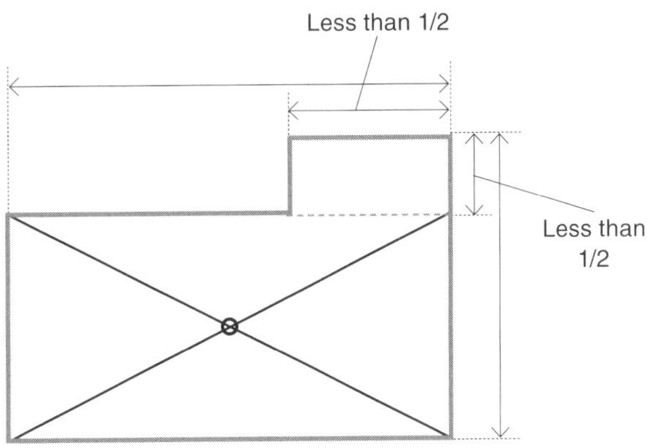

In the event of an "L"-shaped building, treat the center of the rectangle that belongs to the front face of the building as the center of the entire building, and split it into eight sections that way.

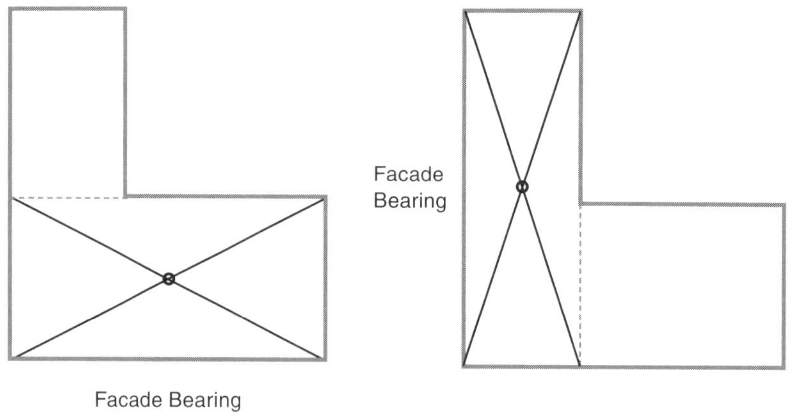

For "C"– or "U"–shaped buildings, draw your lines based on the larger rectangle that the footprint of the building creates, as shown in the diagram below.

*Do not include balconies in determining shape

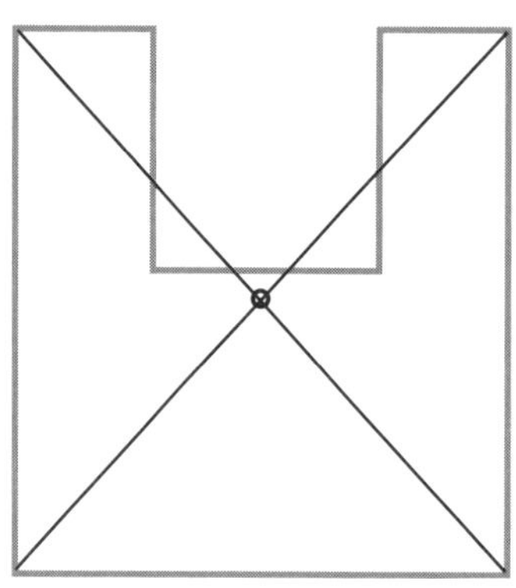

For buildings with sloping walls, like in the figure below, identify the point of the sloping wall that divides its length in two, and draw your diagonal lines based on a rectangle that passes through that point.

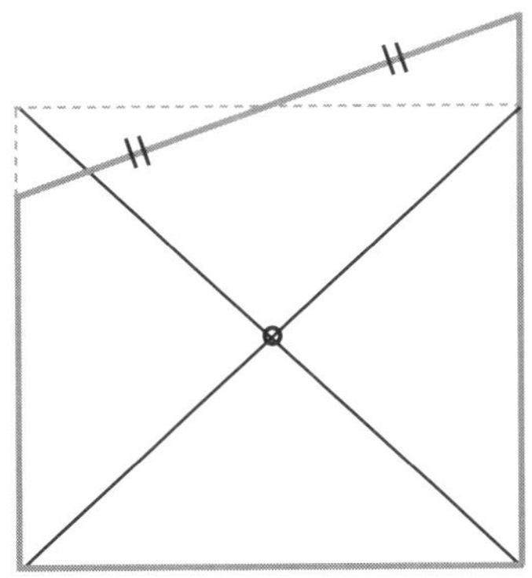

3. Determining the direction in which a building faces: the Facing Direction

This is the most delicate part of feng shui evaluation.
If the direction that the building faces (its Facing Direction) is determined incorrectly, the Flying Star chart will similarly be incorrect, and the entire appraisal process will result in failure. Of course, there are cases where the process is straightforward, but there are also cases where it is quite difficult.

When determining the Facing Direction , the following two points are important.
1. In which direction did the designers of the building intend it to face?
2. From which direction is the building drawing its energy? The Facing Direction can be determined based on the following criteria:

— Entrances
— Open spaces and roads
— Many windows
— Balconies, terraces, etc., with excellent views

The cases where the direction in which entrance faces can be identified as the Facing Direction.
— Building that was designed such that its entrance was intended to be the facing direction.
— There is an open space or garden in front of the entrance.
— Both sides of the building and its rear are directly touching other buildings.
— The entrance faces a road

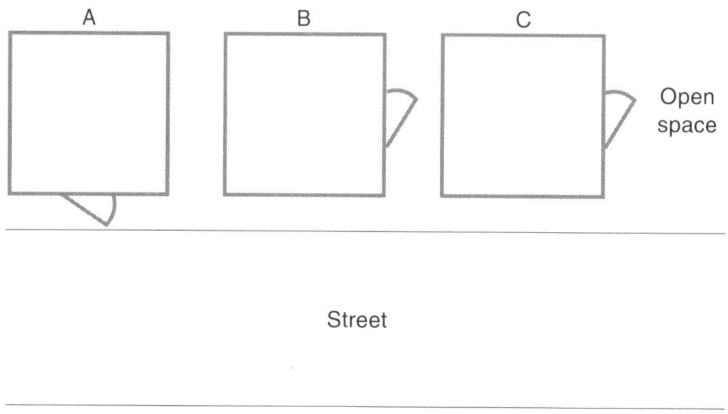

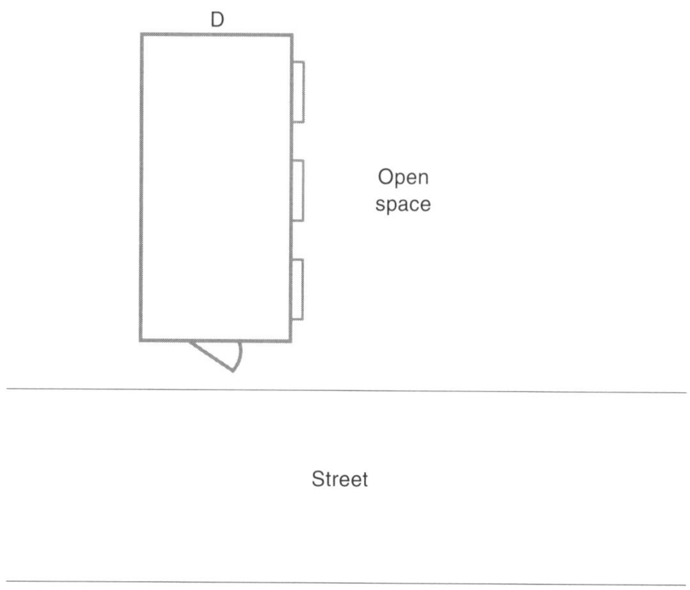

Based on the above, we can imagine that the Facing Direction of Building A is a road side. In the case of Building B, imagine two scenarios. In the first scenario, there is only a small window on the road side (insufficient for taking in energy), but the side with the entrance was designed to be the facade of the building. In this case, the entrance side is the Facing Direction. On the other hand, if Building B had many windows or a balcony, etc., on the side facing the road, this could be considered the intended Facing Direction of the building, such that the Facing Direction of Building B faces the road.

In the case of C and D, the Facing Direction is a competition between the size of the open space and the width and traffic volume of the road, such that it can be difficult to determine the intended design (that is, which side of the building is the Facing Direction).

In the case of buildings on the corner of an intersection, the side with a main entrance that faces the wider, busier road can be appraised as the Facing Direction (such as the case of the ION building in Singapore). If the roads have similar size and traffic, the side with a main entrance and greater residential use can be designated as the facade.

4. Measure the exact direction in which the building faces.

Necessary equipment:

— Compass with degree marks or a smartphone compass

— The most accurate floorplan available

— A ruler and writing implement

— The Direction Division Sheet, in the Appendix

* Face the front of the building in parallel fashion, holding your compass at waist height, parallel to the floor. Align the compass needle so that the needle points north. The direction that points towards you is the Facing Direction. Alternatively, use a smartphone app to achieve the same result.

Front

* In the case of smartphones, North should be set as magnetic north. Both magnetic compasses and smartphone compasses are sensitive to the magnetic fields of the immediate surroundings. This effect is especially pronounced in close proximity to buildings, so it is preferable to take the measurement at a distance from the building, away from cars or metal poles. This will help to ensure an accurate reading.

Front orientation

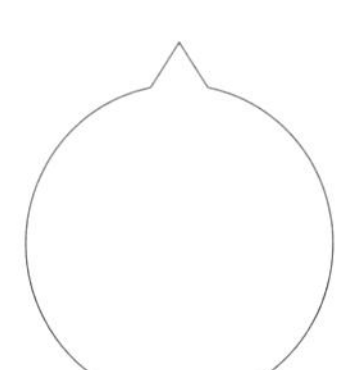

Measurement

Find the directional degree you measured on your compass or smartphone on the Direction Division Sheet in the Appendix. The bearing that contains your measured degree is the Facing Direction of your building (for example, 180 degrees corresponds to Facing Direction South 2).

*Each bearing is split into 45-degree increments, across the eight bearings. Each bearing has three 15-degree subdivisions, but as subdivisions 2 and 3 result in the same chart, there are ultimately only two Flying Star charts for a given bearing. On this basis, a given Age (20 years) has a total of 16 Flying Star charts: 2 subdivisions per bearing, times 8 bearings (see Appendix).

Select the corresponding Flying Star chart (Age 6, Age 7, Age 8, Age 9) from the back of the book.

5. Determining Facing Direction from Maps

Measuring direction by compass or smartphone is easily influenced by surrounding magnetic fields, and there are cases where the correct direction cannot be measured correctly. In particular, it is nearly impossible to take a measurement in urban areas that will not be affected by surrounding magnetic fields, but there is a way to determine the direction using a map. If you are able to locate your building on a map, you can determine its correct Facing Direction. Let's take a look again at the Hemingway House in Key West, Florida, to illustrate this method

A. Using a map that has the Hemingway House on it, draw a line parallel to the street through the center point of the building (red dotted line). Draw a line at right angles to this line. This will be the Facing Direction line.

B. Draw a line on the map representing magnetic north.

i Find the magnetic declination.

Since Flying Star Feng Shui uses magnetic north as its North direction, the North direction on maps (true north) has to be adjusted. For example, in Key West, Florida, magnetic north deviates 5.48 degrees towards the west compared to true north.

In New York City, the deviation is 12.42 degrees to the west, while in Los Angeles, it is 11.44 degrees to the east. In Singapore and other equatorial regions, the deviation is close to 0 degrees.

Source: NOAA, National Centers for Environmental Information https://www.ngdc.noaa.gov/geomag/calculators/magcalc.shtml

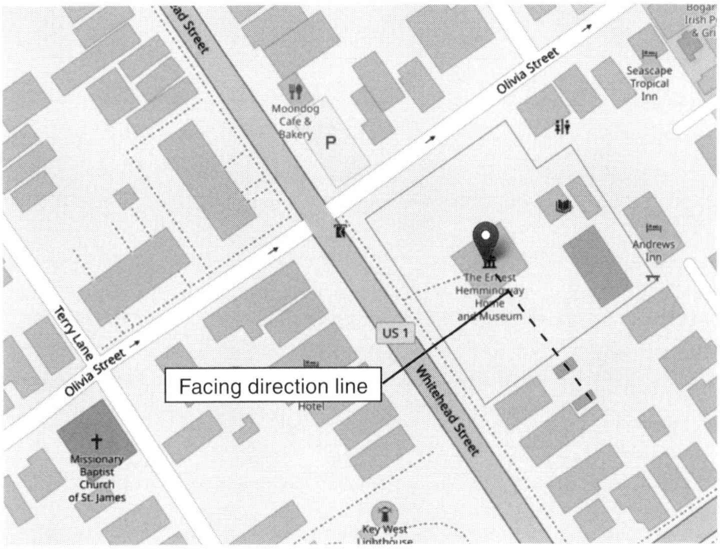

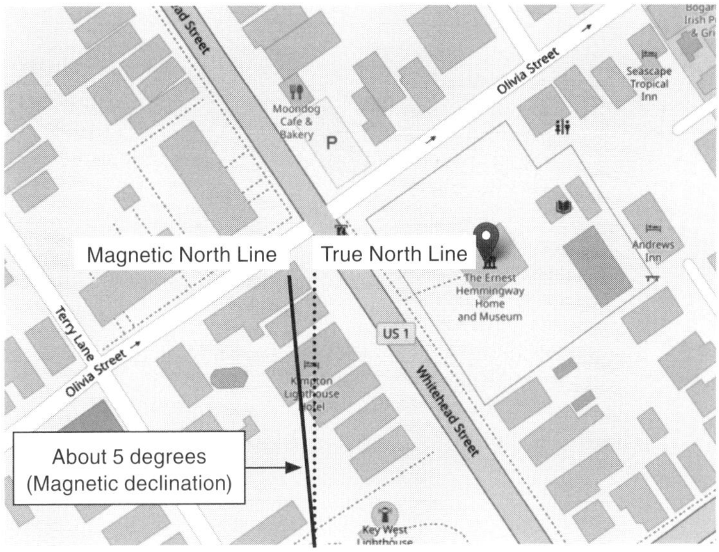

ii For the Hemingway House, we draw a line for true north, and mark a position on the map that is roughly 5 degrees to the west of the origin point of our true north line (this represents the magnetic declination). Draw a line from the origin point of the truth north line to this position. This line represents the magnetic north line.

C. Using triangulation or a set square, draw a second magnetic north line parallel to the original that passes through the origin point of the Facade Bearing line.

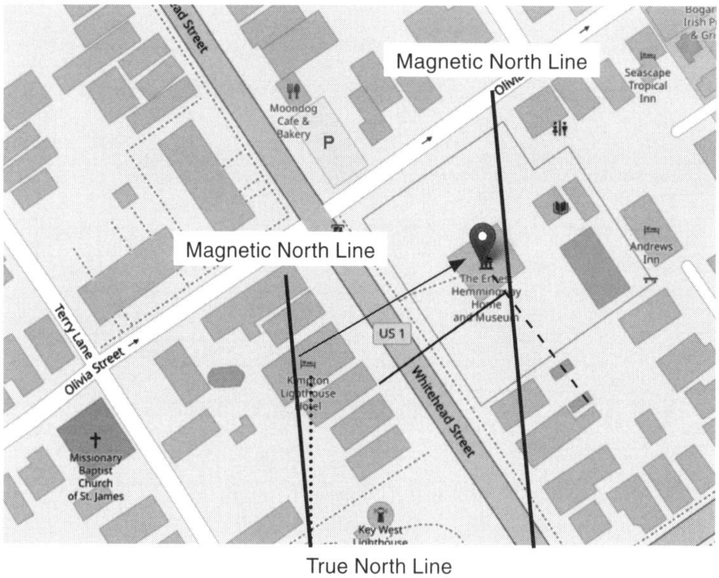

D. Next, we center our protractor over the central point and the origin point of the Facing Direction line. While ensuring that we do not move off this point, we overlap the north–south line of the sheet with the magnetic north line. The bearing that the Facing Direction line lies in becomes the true Facing Direction. In this case, we measure 241 degrees, giving us the Southwest 2–3.

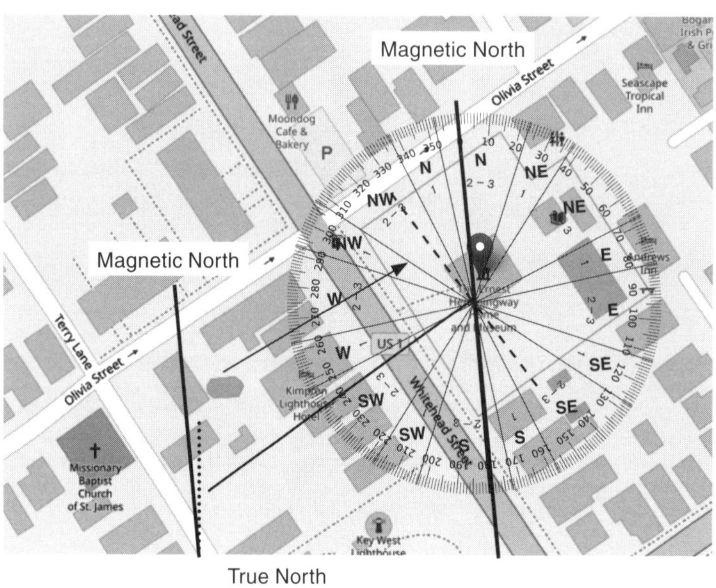

Figure 6: Facing direction line

Upon determining the Facing Direction, we can establish the Hemingway House's Flying Star chart and divide the floorplan into bearings that will reveal its Wealth and Spiritual Stars.

The method for dividing a floorplan into bearings

1. First, we mark the center of the floorplan, and draw a line from that point in the direction of the Facing Direction.

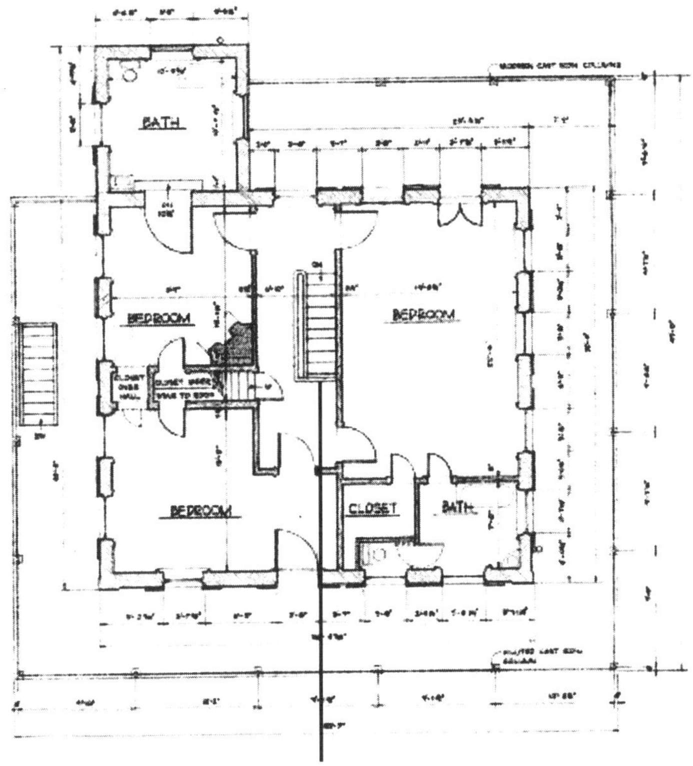

Facing direction line

Figure 7: Facing direction line

2. Next, we center the Direction Division Sheet on the center point of the floorplan. While ensuring that the Sheet remains centered, align the directional degree of the Facing Direction (241 degrees, in this case) with the Facing Direction line. From here, mark off each bearing at 45-degree increments.

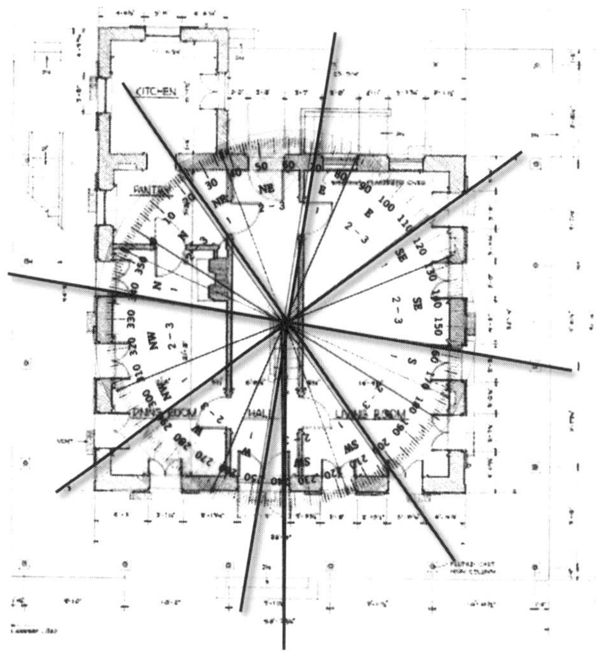

Facing direction line

3. Remove the Direction Division Sheet and draw in the lines.

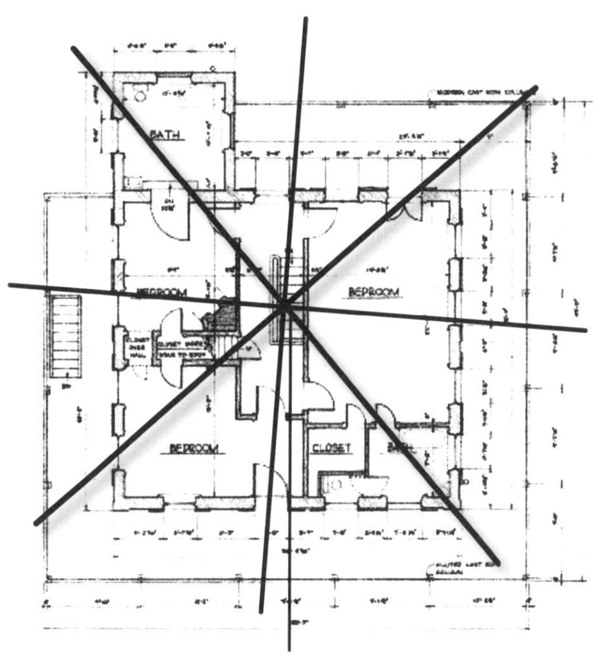

4. Referring to the Flying Star chart, fill in each bearing with its corresponding Spiritual Star (left number) and Wealth Star (right number).

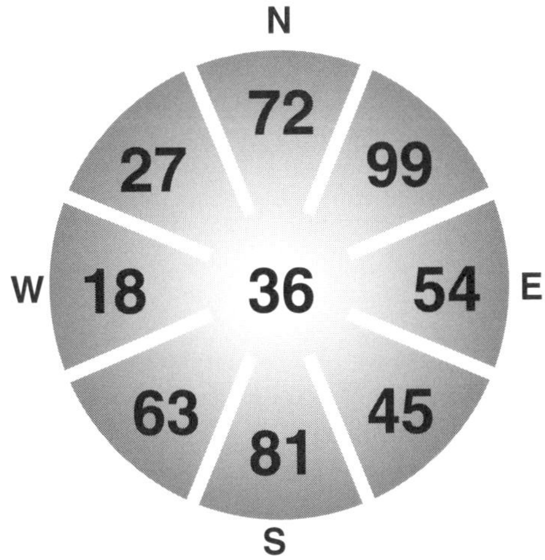

Figure 8: Flying Star Chart

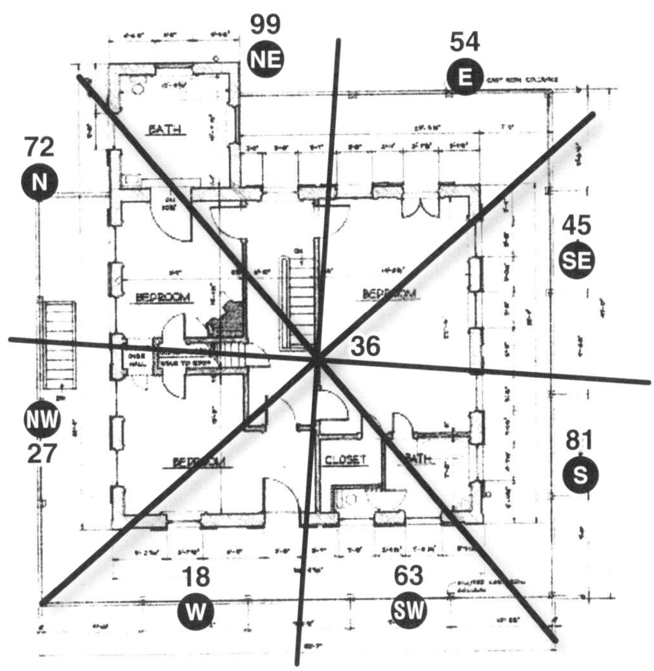

The Way to Evaluate Apartments

1. First, determine the Flying Star chart of the entire apartment building based on the above process.

2. Apply the apartment building's Flying Star chart to your own apartment floorplan to divide it into eight bearings and determine where Wealth Stars and Spiritual Stars are present.

The Way to Evaluate Stores and Offices in Larger Buildings

First, determine the Flying Star chart of the entire building based on the above process.

Apply the building's Flying Star chart to your own store or office floorplan to divide it into eight bearings and determine where Wealth Stars and Spiritual Stars are present.

For example, a cafe in Singapore's ION Building would apply the ION Flying Star chart to its floorplan.

* In the event that a residence, office, or shop has a separate entrance from the main entrance of the building it is in, use a Flying Star chart based on the Facing Direction of that space.

What to Do When Conflicts in Selecting a Chart Arise

Sometimes there are cases where it is difficult to determine the Facing Direction or the Facing Direction is straddling two different bearings, making it difficult to establish which chart to use. There are times where it's difficult for professionals, too.

First, select as many charts as seem appropriate for the Facing Direction. Then, determine where the most Auspicious Wealth Star is for each of them (for the Age that governs 2024–2043, it is Wealth Star 9). Based on the strongest Wealth Stars for each of these maps, move a pendulum clock between their bearings at a frequency of no less and no more than once per month. Carefully monitor changes in economic fortunes between these months in order to determine the bearing that had the greatest effect. The result is your answer. However, as Chapter 5 will explain, we can't use this method when the year star 5 visiting is in the direction 5 alignment in a bearing, as this method will not work.

There is also a way to make a determination based on the bearing of Wealth Star 5. If you are encountering AC, TV, or other appliance difficulties in a bearing that has Wealth Star 5 according to one of your charts, that chart is likely accurate. Similarly, if you have difficulty sleeping in a bedroom, if one of your charts shows that your bedroom is home to Spiritual Star 5, it is likely the correct one.

Chapter 4

Improving Health and Financial Fortune with Flying Star Feng Shui

Check the Bearing of Wealth Star 9

Once you have split your floorplan into bearings and filled in their Wealth and Spiritual Stars, note the bearing that contains Wealth Star 9.

If the bearing with Wealth Star 9 contains an entrance, expansive views, windows facing a road, a living room, dining room, staircase, atrium, elevator, or escalator, the people living in that building will be blessed with financial fortune during Age 9. Using some of the methods for reinforcing the effect of Wealth Star 9 described below, this good fortune can be strengthened even further.

Wealth Star 9 in the Kitchen

If the kitchen is frequently used, the Star's effect will be activated. If it is not used often, then decorate with a pendulum clock or a similar item that strengthens Wealth Star 9, as described below.

Wealth Star 9 in the Bedroom

This location is unlikely to bring about financial luck. Solar-powered gadgets and the like will at least ensure the Wealth Star is activated during the day. Alternatively, activate Wealth Star 1 using the methods described below.

Wealth Star 9 in a WC or Bathroom

This location is unlikely to bring about financial luck. If there is space, try decorating with items that enhance Wealth Star 9. Alternatively, activate Wealth Star 1 using the methods described below.

Wealth Star 9 in the Center

This location is unlikely to bring about financial luck in Age 9. If there is space, try decorating with items that enhance Wealth Star 9. Alternatively, activate Wealth Star 1 using the methods described below.

Items to Strengthen Wealth Star 9, Lucky Colors, and Colors to Avoid

Strengthening Items: pendulum clocks, indoor fountains, ikebana *(Japanese flower arranging)*, aquatic plants like lucky bamboo, saltwater, wooden objects

Lucky Colors: red, orange, pink, purple, blue, green, black, gray

Colors to Avoid: white, gold, silver, brown, yellow, beige

Items to Strengthen Wealth Star 1, Lucky Colors, and Colors to Avoid

Strengthening Items: pendulum clocks, indoor fountains, crystals and rocks, ceramics, metal objects

Lucky Colors: black, gray, white, gold, silver, brown, yellow, beige

Colors to Avoid: red, orange, pink, purple, green, blue

Wealth Stars 2–8 in Entrances, Living Rooms, Kitchens, and Staircases

If an entrance, living room, dining room, kitchen, or staircase contains Wealth Stars 2–8, consider the following countermeasures. If these inauspicious stars are in a bathroom, WC, storehouse, or similar, no countermeasures are necessary.

The Effects of Wealth Star 2, Items to Counter It, Lucky Colors, and Colors to Avoid

Effects: may invite illness

Countermeasure Items: placement of 6 metal coins (any metal or color). You may put them under a rug or carpet.

Lucky Colors: white, black, gray, gold, silver

Colors to Avoid: red, orange, pink, purple, blue, green, yellow, brown, beige

The Effects of Wealth Star 3, Items to Counter It, Lucky Colors, and Colors to Avoid

Effects: may invite arguments, fights, and burglaries

Countermeasure Items: red cloth, paper, and ceramics

Lucky Colors: red, orange, pink, purple, yellow, brown, beige

Colors to Avoid: blue, green, black, gray, white, gold, silver

The Effects of Wealth Star 4, Items to Counter It, Lucky Colors, and Colors to Avoid

Effects: may invite sexual scandals and other forms of trouble

Countermeasure Items: red cloth, paper, and ceramics

Lucky Colors: red, orange, pink, purple, yellow, brown, beige

Colors to Avoid: blue, green, black, gray, white, gold, silver

The Effects of Wealth Star 5, Items to Counter It, Lucky Colors, and Colors to Avoid

Effects: May invite misfortune. the most inauspicious star among the 9 stars.

Countermeasure Items: Metal wind chime on places such as door knobs or curtain hooks (the type that makes sound as a result of metal hitting metal) so that they make sound upon opening or closing, or saltwater in a glass bottle.

Lucky Colors: black, gray, white, gold, silver

Colors to Avoid: red, orange, pink, purple, yellow, brown, beige, blue, green

The Effects of Wealth Star 6, Items to Counter It, Lucky Colors, and Colors to Avoid

Effects: may invite legal troubles

Countermeasure Items: placement of three aquatic plants such as lucky bamboo, or vinegar in a glass bottle

Lucky Colors: blue, green, black, gray

Colors to Avoid: white, gold, silver, red, orange, pink, purple, yellow, brown, beige

The Effects of Wealth Star 7, Items to Counter It, Lucky Colors, and Colors to Avoid

Effects: may invite legal troubles and careless remarks

Countermeasure Items: placement of three aquatic plants such as lucky bamboo, or vinegar in a glass bottle

Lucky Colors: blue, green, black, gray

Colors to Avoid: white, gold, silver, red, orange, pink, purple, yellow, brown, beige

The Effects of Wealth Star 8, Items to Counter It, Lucky Colors, and Colors to Avoid

Effects: may invite misfortune on boys and young males

Countermeasure Items: placement of metal wind chimes on places such as door knobs or curtain hooks (the type that makes sound as a result of metal hitting metal) so that they make sound upon opening or closing, or saltwater in a glass bottle.

Lucky Colors: black, gray, white, gold, silver

Colors to Avoid: red, orange, pink, purple, yellow, brown, beige, blue, green

Check the Bearing of Spiritual Star 9

In contrast to Wealth Stars, which are activated by open, active environments, Spiritual Stars are activated in quiet spaces.

In Age 9 (2024–2043)

Home | The bearing with Spiritual Star 9 is the best place for a bedroom or study.
The bearing with Spiritual Star 1 is the second-best place for a bedroom or study.

Office | The bearing with Spiritual Star 9 is the best place for an executive or administrative office (or chair).
The bearing with Spiritual Star 1 is the second-best place for an executive or administrative office (or chair).

Shop | The bearing with Spiritual Star 9 is the best place for a cash register.
The bearing with Spiritual Star 1 is the second-best place for a cash register.

In order to strengthen the energy of auspicious Spiritual Stars, it is best to avoid using electrical appliances and to be quiet in the room. Also, if a room has large windows or windows facing a body of water or a pool, this will also weaken the energy of the Spiritual Star.

Items to Strengthen Spiritual Star 9, Lucky Colors, and Colors to Avoid

Strengthening Items: ikebana, aquatic plants, saltwater, wooden objects
Lucky Colors: red, orange, pink, purple, blue, green, black, gray
Colors to Avoid: white, gold, silver, brown, yellow, beige

Items to Strengthen Spiritual Star 1, Lucky Colors, and Colors to Avoid

Strengthening Items: crystals and rocks, ceramics, metal objects, saltwater
Lucky Colors: black, gray, white, gold, silver, brown, yellow, beige
Colors to Avoid: red, orange, pink, purple, green, blue

The ways to weaken inauspicious Spiritual Stars 2–8 in bedrooms, studies, executive offices/desks, and cash registers are the same as those for Wealth Stars 2–8.

Feng Shui Evaluation: A Case Study of an Apartment

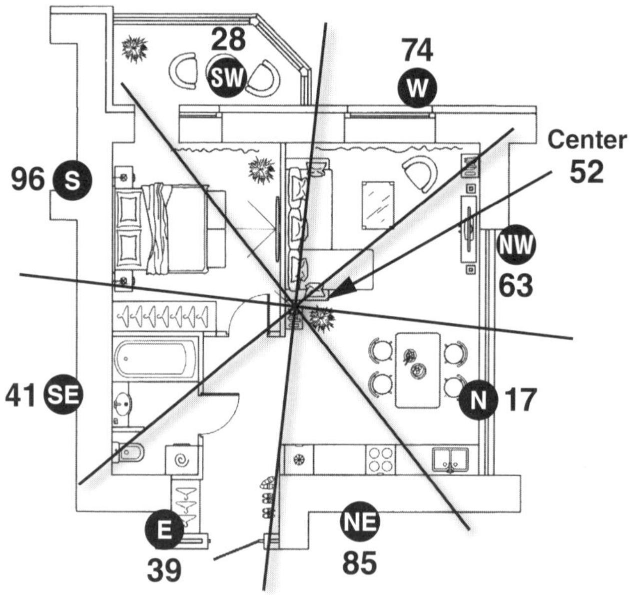

Figure 9: Age 8 Facing Direction Northeast 2–3

Here is how to approach an Age 8, Facing Direction Northeast 2–3 apartment with flying star feng shui.

East (Entrance)

As Wealth Star 9 is present here, this entrance will provide financial fortune until 2023. Wealth Star 9 can be strengthened here by decorating around the entrance with its lucky colors: red, orange, pink, purple, black, gray, blue, and green.

Northeast (Kitchen)

The stove area of the kitchen is visited by the most inauspicious Wealth Star 5, which invites bad luck and disaster. This can be addressed by setting a glass bottle of saltwater or metal wind chimes on a cupboard or door that will make noise when opening or closing.

North (Dining)

Wealth Star 7 is present here. In order to defend against legal problems and scandals, place three lucky bamboo plants or a glass bottle of vinegar in the room. Lucky colors shared with the kitchen to the northeast are black and gray.

Northwest (Living)

In order to deal with Wealth Star 3, which invites arguments and thefts, incorporate red cloth or paper, or ceramics. It is best not to keep flowers in this bearing (including plants). Lucky colors are red, orange, pink, purple, brown, and yellow.

West (Living)

Wealth Star 4 is present here, which invites issues in sexual relations. It is best not to keep flowers in this bearing (including plants). This bearing shares lucky colors of red and brown with the northwest.

Southwest

Wealth Star 8 is present in this bearing, which contains a balcony and door. The opening and closing of this door activated financial fortune in Age 8, but from 2024, the star will be in decline. This may cause problems for young men who choose to live here, which can be cured by attaching metal wind chimes to the doorknob of the door.

South (Bedroom)

Spiritual Star 9 is present in this bedroom. In Age 9, this is the best possible situation for a bedroom. Lucky colors are red, orange, pink, purple, black, gray, blue, and green.

Southeast (Bathroom)

Wealth Star 1 is present. Starting in 2044, Wealth Star 1 will be the most auspicious Wealth Star, but won't be of much use in a bathroom without windows.

Conclusion

In Age 9, the current age, the entrance and bedroom of this apartment are both blessed by the most auspicious stars, making this an excellent abode from a feng shui perspective.

Beginning in Age 1 (2044–2063), the Wealth Star 9 of the entrance and Spiritual Star 9 of the bedroom will be in decline. The most auspicious Spiritual Star, Spiritual Star 1, will be present in the dining room, which cannot be used as a bedroom, while the second most auspicious Wealth Star, Wealth Star 2, will be in the center bearing and difficult to activate. This apartment is difficult to recommend for Age 1 residence.

Chapter 5

Flying Stars That Change Position Yearly and their Countermeasures

So far, we have looked at how to determine and interpret Flying Star charts, but there are actually some feng shui techniques that do not require Flying Star charts, but only the process of designating the eight bearings of a building as described in Chapter 3.

The appraisal process is quite simple, but very importantly, the techniques this process affords are sufficient to minimize the likelihood of the worst of calamities.

In any building, there are nine stars that change their positions every year in a manner that is not depicted by the Wealth Star and Spiritual Star layout of the Flying Star chart.

These stars are called the Year Stars.

These stars exert the same influence on the other stars, whether it is a Wealth Star in an entrance or a Spiritual Star in a bedroom. Even if the Wealth Star in an entrance is Wealth Star 9 during an auspicious Age, if the Year Star in that bearing is inauspicious, some caution is warranted for the year in which it is there.

There are nine Year Stars, but you need only worry about the following:
Year Star 2: Illness
Year Star 3: Argument, conflict, crimes such as burglary
Year Star 5: The most inauspicious star, inconvenience, calamity, fatally bad luck
Year Star 7: Legal issues, scandals, incriminating remarks

Year Star 4 and Year Star 6 are mild in terms of their negative effects and should not be a source of concern.

Year Stars in the center bearing can be ignored unless the bearing contains a staircase or a room with high traffic or occupation.

The Year Stars change their position every year on the first day of the Lichun according to the Chinese calendar. (see page 48)

Countermeasures for Year Star 5, Bringer of Bad Luck, Calamity, and Danger

Of all nine Year Stars, this is the one that requires the most attention.
Even in a bearing with auspicious Wealth or Spiritual Star, if it has important places like entrances, desks, cash registers, and bedrooms in a year when Fortune Star 5 is active there, caution is required.

Aside from entrances, if a location in the auspicious Wealth Star bearing is decorated with pendulum clocks, indoor fountains, houseplants, etc. in order to activate its energy, the decorations should be removed in a year when Year Star 5 is active there.

To deal with this star, place metal wind chimes on door knobs and similar places in the area, and make them ring from time to time. What matters is the sound of metal on metal: cast-iron chimes are fine, any metal material is fine, as long as it's metal.

Place chimes in any area that this Year Star affects–whether it be an entrance, desk, register, living room, or bedroom–and keep them there for the entire year.

Recommended colors for affected areas during this year are white, black, gray, gold, and silver.

The countermeasures that follow are the same as those described in Chapter 4.

Countermeasures for Year Star 2, Bringer of Illness

Place 6 metal coins somewhere in the affected area. They do not need to be visible, so it is sufficient to place them out of sight, such as under a carpet.

Countermeasures for Year Star 3, Bringer of Conflict and Crime:

Place red paper in the affected area. Red rugs, curtains, or ceramics will also work.

Countermeasures for Year Star 7, Bringer of Legal Troubles and Scandals

Place three or four plants that can thrive in water alone somewhere in the affected area. The quintessential example is lucky bamboo, but any plant that requires only water will suffice.

If the plant is in bad health, replace it immediately. Another option is vinegar in a glass bottle.

* There is no need to remove items intended to enhance or counteract the main Flying Stars of a building. For example, if an entrance visited by Wealth Star 7 has lucky bamboo in it, it need not be removed on a year when Year Star 3, for example, inhabits that bearing. Instead, simply add the regular Year Star 3 countermeasures to the space (red ceramics, etc.).

Year Star (2023 Lichun–Before the day 2032 Lichun)

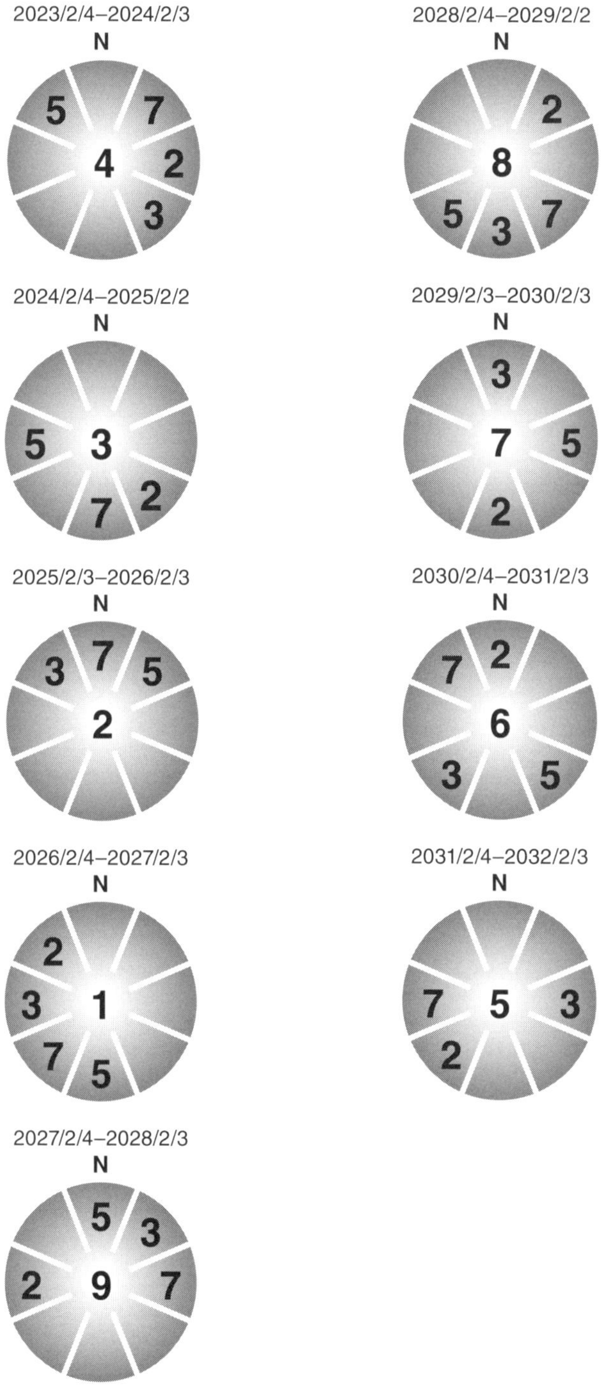

Figure 10: Year Star (2023 Lichun–Before the day 2032 Lichun)

The End-of-Century Misfortune that Befell the Austrian Imperial Family

There are quite a few cases where it is difficult to read the fates of those living in imperial or royal palaces in terms of Flying Star feng shui. In cases where these grand buildings were built up from what were originally hunting outposts or fortifications over the course of repeated renovations, it is a challenge to determine which Age truly represents the building. It can also be difficult to determine the parts of the building in which the members of the royal family were actually active.

While it is difficult to create an accurate Flying Star chart in these instances, certain appraisals are possible by investigating the annual effects of the Year Stars as they move through the bearings of the building.

From the end of the 19th century to the start of the 20th, the reigning family of the Austro-Hungarian Empire would spend their summers at Schönbrunn Palace. The family of Franz Joseph I stayed in the apartments in the west wing of the palace. In 1918, Carl I (the last Austro-Hungarian emperor) defected abroad, putting an end to the Habsburg reign—but until that point, there were a number of foreboding episodes that may have shaken the stability of the family. As mentioned earlier in this book, the original heir to the throne, Rudolf, died in a suicide pact with his lover in 1889 (assassination theories also exist). In 1898, Empress Elisabeth was assassinated while abroad in Switzerland, and in 1916, the 68-year reign of Franz Joseph I, the long-standing figurehead of the empire, came to an end with his death. In every single one of these years, Year Star 5, the most inauspicious star, occupied the west wing apartments of the summer palace of the imperial family.

1889 Crown Prince Rudolf's lover double-suicide

1898 Empress Elisabeth is assassinated in Switzerland

1916 Emperor Franz Joseph I dies

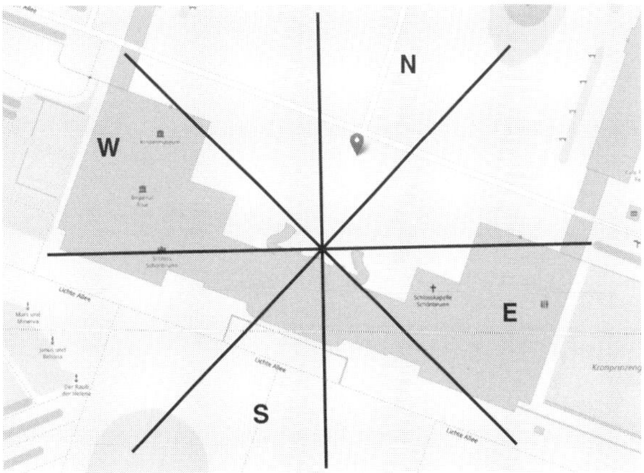

Figure 11: Schönbrunn Palace

Chapter 6

The Effects of the Auspicious Wealth Star

Singapore—The City Where a Feng Shui Master Determines the Position of the Entrance of the Building

This is a country with a harmonious balance of greenery and ultra-contemporary skyscrapers–and while it's not obvious, feng shui has been infused into its buildings. Of course, I don't mean the obvious feng shui principles one can see embedded in the city's commercialist attractions, such as in the Merlions, the Singapore Flyer (a ferris wheel), or the extravagant fountains in Suntec City. I'm talking about Flying Star Feng Shui, manipulating the energies you *can't* see.

In 2015, a leading figure in the founding of Singapore passed away: former Prime Minister Lee Kuan Yew. When Singapore, a small island at the tip of the Malaysian peninsula, was forcibly made independent in 1965, it was little more than a poor emerging economy of ethnic Chinese, Malaysians, and Indians, with no common language or religion. This cramped parcel of land had no natural resources–even needing to get its supply of drinking water from foreign nations–and yet it has transformed itself into what is today, in the 21st century, a wealthy nation with the highest GDP per capita in Asia. The driving force behind this change is widely considered to be Lee Kuan Yew's outstanding ability and, for better or for worse, his iron-fisted style of government–but I think it is impossible to deny that some of this nation's economic prosperity was due to the widespread consultation of feng shui practitioners by the ethnic Chinese entrepreneurs who managed hotels, shopping malls, offices, and residences.

As the examples presented below are all commercial establishments, the focus will be on the Wealth Star, which affects financial prosperity.

ION (2009–)

ION (2009–)

On the corner of the intersection of Orchard Road and Scotts Road is a large shopping mall called ION. It is an enormous structure that cannot be conveyed by a single picture.

The use of Flying Star Feng Shui techniques in this building is so masterful that I cannot help but include some of the details into this text, which will demonstrate the basics of employing the Wealth Star in order to enhance financial prosperity.

This building has an Age 8 flying star chart, facing towards the northeast 1. The following shows its Wealth Star chart, in which only the Wealth Stars have been included.

Figure 12: Ion's Wealth Star Chart, Age 8, Facing Northeast 1

The main entrances of this huge shopping mall contain Wealth Star 8 (in the northeast), the most powerful Wealth Star of the current Age, and while it's still a long way off, Wealth Star 1 (in the northwest), the most powerful Wealth Star of the Age from 2044 to 2063.

Wealth Star 9, which will offer prosperity in the 20-year period that will begin in 2024, is located in the west bearing, which is not directly visible from Orchard Road. While the entrance here is small, the food court, which is the most active, crowded part of the mall, and the escalator that runs from the 4th basement floor to the 1st floor, fully activate the area.

ION

Wealth Star 9: this escalator runs from the 1st floor to the 4th floor of the basement, revealing the food court located there.

A Collaboration Between Visible and Invisible Energies

This shopping mall is meticulously planned in a manner that goes well beyond its placement of auspicious Wealth Stars at entrances. The southwest bearing, opposite to the bearing towards which the building faces, contains inauspicious Wealth Star 5. Due to the presence of a taxi stand in this bearing, Wealth Star 5 can be somewhat revitalized by the taxi activity. To seal the energy of the Wealth Star 5, they activate the energy of the Spiritual Star 8 by placing a high rise condominium in this bearing. While Spiritual Star 8 is only auspicious until 2023, because ION is a commercial establishment, there is great merit to focusing more on stopping the activity of Wealth Star 5.

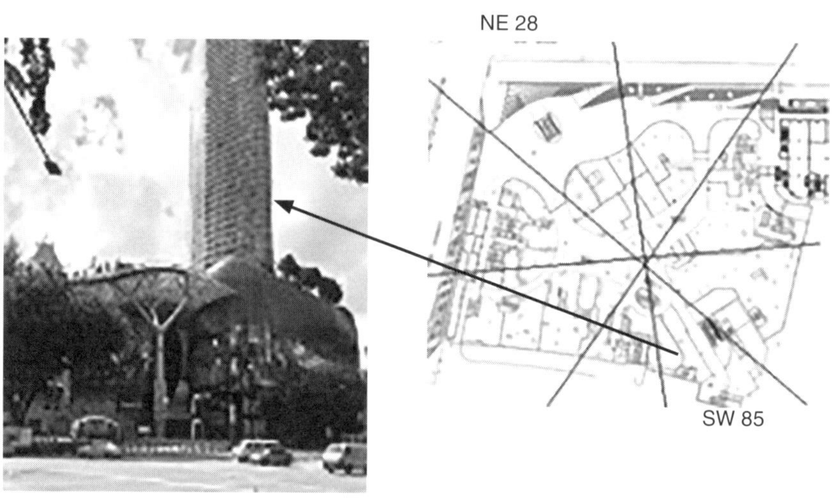

Figure 13: Left, ION seen from a distance (2016, the author). Right, ION's floorplan

Shangri-La Hotel (1971–)

The Shangri-La Hotel is a venerable fixture of the city that, since its establishment in 1971, has practically acted as the official reception hall of Singapore.

It is host to national days sponsored by the embassies of numerous nations, and is frequently used for international conferences such as the Shangri-La Dialogue, attended by dignitaries from countries across the globe.

It is the flagship establishment of Shangri-La Hotels and Resorts, owned by the Malaysian-born business magnate Robert Kuok.

Shangri-La Hotel (1971–)

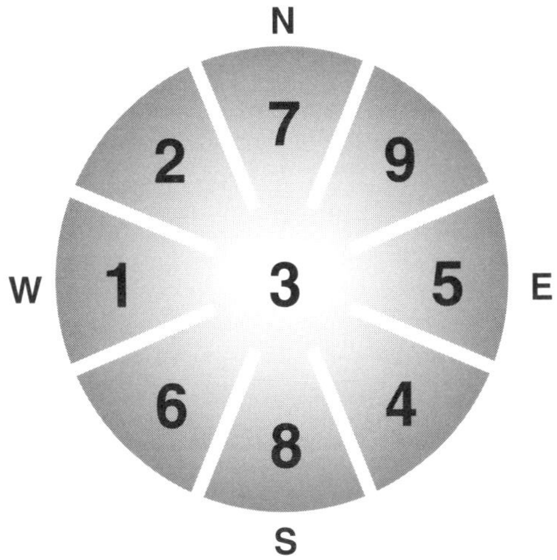

Figure 14: Wealth Star Chart of Shangri-La Hotel (Age 6, Facing Southwest 2–3)

While this may be an apocryphal story, it is said that the mother of Robert Kuok–who amassed his fortune in the space of a single generation–would inspect the hotel with feng shui consultants every year, just before Chinese New Year.

Age 6 (establishment–1983): Main Entrance, Wealth Star 6
Age 7 (1984–2003): Pool, Wealth Star 7
Age 8 (2004–2023): Ballroom Entrance, Wealth Star 8
Age 9 (2024–2043): Tower Wing, Garden Side, Wealth Star 9
Age 1 (2044–2063): Pond with a waterfall, Wealth Star 1

Looking at the map, it seems that the Valley Wing disturbs the view of the Tower Wing, but there is actually a fair amount of distance between these buildings, and as the Tower Wing is built on slightly lower ground, the north view of the Tower Wing was designed to be quite impressive.

Grand Hotel Wien

The Grand Hotel Wien could be described as a living example of a building that accords with the theory of Flying Star Feng Shui.

In 2010, the Grand Hotel in Vienna, the capital of Austria, reached its 140th founding anniversary. Surviving both the final days of the Austro-Hungarian Empire at the end of the 19th century and the chaos of World War I and World War II, the outward appearance of the hotel today is no different than how it looked in the year it was established, 1870. However, from the perspective of Flying Star Feng Shui, the charts of the hotel at its founding and today are totally different. Let's take a look at the past and present of this hotel, an icon of Vienna.

Before the opening of the 1873 World's Fair in Vienna, then the capital of the Austro-Hungarian Empire, there was a hotel-building rush underway in preparation for visitors. The Rathaus (City Hall) and the Vienna State Opera were also being built at this time.

In 1865, a certain Mr. Schneider completed work on a personal home he began building in 1861, but from the beginning, he intended to remodel it into a hotel. The renovations began in 1866 and were completed in 1870.

Therefore, in Flying Star Feng Shui, this building belongs to Age 1 (1864–1883).

The hotel became popular–to the point of being difficult to get a reservation–immediately after it opened. In 1911, the hotel was expanded to a building twice the size, and subsequently survived two world wars. After WWII, it briefly became the headquarters of the international institution, IAEA, but in 1991, it was purchased by ANA (All Nippon Airways). After this purchase, all but one of the outer walls was demolished, the building was rebuilt according to its original dimensions and appearance, and was reborn as the Grand Hotel it is today. In Flying Star Feng Shui, if a building is torn down leaving only a single wall, even if the outside appearance is the same, the structure is treated as a new building henceforth. Thus, the Grand Hotel Wien of today has a completely different flying star chart than the one used to analyze it in this book.

The hotel in 1870, its founding year

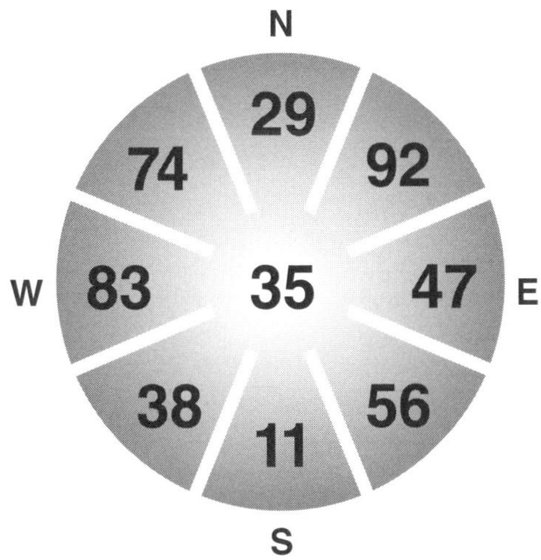

Figure 15: Flying star chart of the Grand Hotel Wien (Age 1, Facing South 2–3)

Bearing numbers:

Left: Spiritual Star

Right: Wealth Star

Example: North bearing, 2 Spiritual Star, 9 Wealth Star

As this is a commercial establishment, we'll only look at the Wealth Stars.

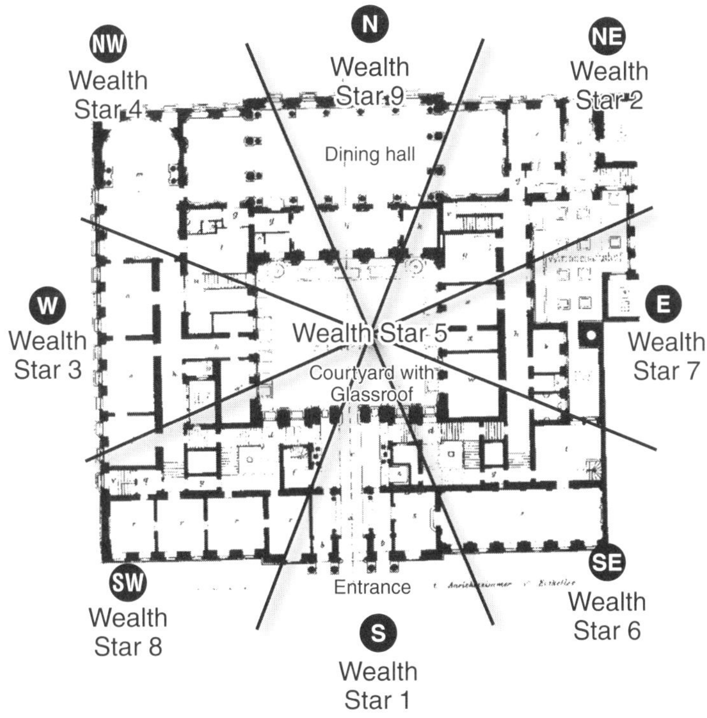

Figure 16: The Original First Floor Floorplan of the Grand Hotel

Kärntner Ring, Wealth Star 1 Entrance

Wealth Star 3, west side windows

1911 (Age 3) expansion

Wealth Star 4, dining hall

Age 1 1864–1883 Most auspicious star: Wealth Star 1

Location: entrance (south)

The hotel was established in 1870, with 300 guest rooms, a steam-powered elevator, and a telegraph office, quickly achieving popularity as a cutting-edge, top-class luxury hotel. The elevator resulted in the 2nd floor becoming popular, a floor which in past hotels would be used by servants alone.

Age 2 1884–1903 Most auspicious star: Wealth Star 2

Location: rear entrance on Maximilian Street (northeast)

Part of the dining hall. Maximilian Street (now Mahler Street) was, at that time, a gathering point for fiaker (horse-drawn carriages) for hotel guests; along with other carts that appeared there, it was a lively street.

The hotel became the center of Vienna high society.

At this time, Johann Strauss was a superstar in the music world. His younger brother, Eduard Strauss, regularly conducted performances at the hotel. In 1894, over 200 celebrities attended a concert celebrating Johann Strauss' 50th birthday–not least of whom was Johannes Brahms. Other regular patrons included individuals linked to the Hapsburgs. The niece of Empress Elisabeth, Countess Larisch von Moennich, made the Grand Hotel her usual lodging; she is said to have later been involved in arranging the clandestine meeting between Crown Prince Rudolf and Baroness Mary Vetsera, which resulted in their deaths by suicide pact. As the story goes, Mary Vetsera used the back entrance to board a carriage bound for Mayerling, the site of the incident.

Age 3 1904–1923 Most auspicious star: Wealth Star 3

Location: along the windows facing Academy Street (west)

In 1911, after great financial success, the adjacent buildings on Kärtner Ring 11 and 13 were purchased and were combined into the hotel, adding 100 more guest rooms. As a result, the distribution of energy throughout the hotel as a whole changed, but the position of Wealth Star 3 was almost unaffected.

In 1914, three years after the expansion, Archduke Franz Ferdinand and his wife were assassinated in Sarajevo, which led to the outbreak of World War I. A gala dinner that had been held in the same year would prove to be the last party hosted by the Hapsburg-Lorraine family as rulers. At the end of the war in 1918, the last Hapsburg emperor, Charles I, abdicated the throne, ending nearly 600 years of Hapsburg rule.

Age 4 1924–1943 Most auspicious star: Wealth Star 4

Location: dining hall, after the addition (northwest)

Also, windows facing Maximilian Street, back entrance

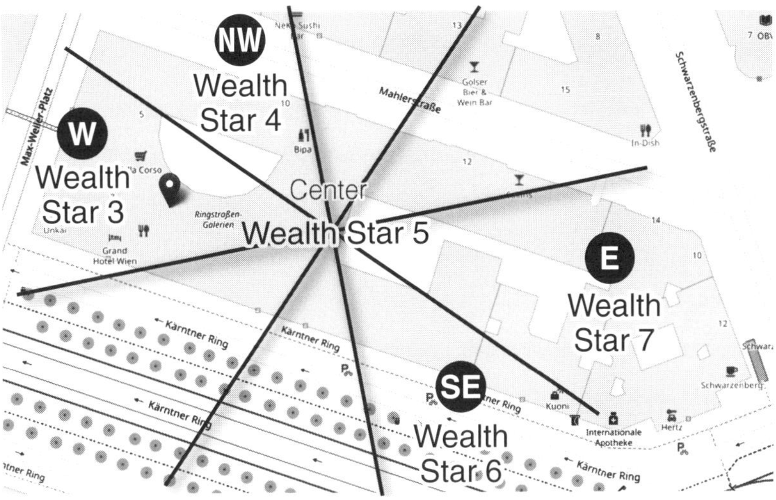

Figure 17: Bearings for Wealth Stars 3, 4, 5, 6, 7 in Grand Hotel, post-expansion

This is a modern map, due to difficulty in locating a historical map for the period.

After World War I was the 1920s–the "Roaring Twenties," as the decade is known in the US. The economic excesses of this period affected the cosmopolitan city of Vienna as well. People were coming into fortunes nearly overnight, and while the waltz had been abandoned in favor of the Charleston, the lifestyle of the upper class returned to its common mode. At this time, the American jazz singer Josephine Baker was enjoying great popularity in Paris, and when she performed in Vienna, she, too, was a guest at the Grand Hotel.

The grill room at the Grand Hotel was always full of people, who would gather there after operas, concerts, and plays. For performers, the hotel was like a second home. The composer Pietro Mascagni and the conductor Wilhelm Furtwängler were known to be guests.

However, this was also a period when the shadows of the Gestapo–the secret police of the Nazis–were growing larger and darker. In 1938, Germany declared its annexation of Austria, which it controlled for seven years. In 1939, Germany's invasion of Poland incited the start of World War II. Throughout this period, the clientele of the hotel was predominantly Nazi officers, but it continued operations as usual.

Age 5 1944–1963 Most auspicious star: Wealth Star 5

Location: Center

After the addition, the center bearing of the hotel had no courtyard or similar space, and thus Wealth Star 5 was inactive. This was the first period during which the most auspicious Wealth Star of the age was inactive in the building.
(see Map A)

In 1945, World War II came to an end. Just before hostilities ceased, Vienna was subjected to an air raid that damaged the Vienna State Opera and St. Stephen's Cathedral, but the hotel was unharmed. Consequently, it fell under the post-war control of the Soviets for 10 years.

In 1955, the Soviet army withdrew, and Austria–and the Grand Hotel–finally regained freedom. Two years later, after the completion of renovations, the hotel was reopened–yet just a year later, the hotel was acquired by the Austrian government and provided on loan to the IAEA.

This was the first time since the hotel's founding that the most auspicious Wealth Star was completely unable to express its effect. The vicissitudes of history had, for a time, brought this hotel's extravagant history to a close.

Age 6 1964–1983 Most auspicious star: Wealth Star 6

Location: Windows on addition portion, facing the Kärtner Ring (southeast)

Until 1979, the building was the headquarters of the IAEA (International Atomic Energy Agency).

Age 7 1984–2003 Most auspicious star: Wealth Star 7

Location: blocked by a building on Kärtner Ring 15 (east)

The most auspicious Wealth Star couldn't be active again since Age 5. After the IAEA left the building in 1979, it was used as a bank for a time, but was purchased by ANA (All Nippon Airways) Holdings in 1991. In 1994, all but the facade of the building was demolished and rebuilt, maintaining only the size and exterior appearance of the original building. Its flying star chart is completely different, and in that sense, it has been reborn as a different building. From the perspective of Flying Star Feng Shui, the hotel that had survived since its Age 1 founding was, at that point, gone forever.

In 2002, JJW Hotels and Resorts bought the ANA Grand Hotel, and renamed it "Grand Hotel Wien."

[Grand Hotel Vienna] by Andreas Augustin was consulted for the section above.

Additional Information

Regarding Grand Hotel Wien

ANA Grand Hotel Wien, Andreas Augustin

The History of Grand Hotel Wien

https://www.grandhotelwien.com/en/about-us/history/

Photo https://www.grandhotelwien.com/en/about-us/history/

Grand Hotel Floorplan

Allgemeine Bauzeitung Wikisource

Map

https://www.openstreetmap.org/?mlat=48.202194&mlon=16.372139&zoom=18#map=19/48.20219/16.37253

Chapter 7

The Effect of the Auspicious Spiritual Star

Quote [1]:

I consider that there are two forms of dreams, and only two, the experiences of the released spirit, and the confused action of the lower faculties which remain in the body when the spirit is absent. The former is rare and beautiful, for the memory of it fails us.

Quote [2]:

401. During sleep does the soul rest like the body?

"No, the spirit is never inactive. During sleep, the bonds that link him to the body are loosened, and as the body does not need him while sleeping, the spirit travels through space and enters into a more direct connection with other spirits."

In contrast to the relative ease with which evidence of the effect of Wealth Stars can be found based on the prosperity of commercial establishments, the Spiritual Stars, which harmonize health and relationships via spaces like bedrooms and studies, have a subjective effect which is difficult to demonstrate with concrete examples. I have personal experience with sleeping better in bearings with auspicious Spiritual Stars, but this is still, ultimately, just the impression of one individual.

If we take it as true that while sleeping, our spirits enter the spirit realm and interact with other spirits, then perhaps we might hypothesize that sleeping in places with auspicious Spiritual Stars enables connection with spirits of a "higher order" (we might call them guardian angels).

I've done some research into what sorts of effects that the serene energy of Spiritual Stars has on people, as well as into the studies and bedrooms of people engaged in work that depends on inspiration.

The Study in which Natsume Sōseki wrote I Am A Cat

Natsume Sōseki lived in a house in the Sendagi neighborhood of Tokyo for about four years, from ages 36 to 39. This house, which is famous as the "birthplace" of the bestselling novel I Am A Cat, has since been dismantled and rebuilt in Meiji-mura in Aichi Prefecture.

The house is also known for being inhabited by Ogai Mori (novelist) for about a year and a half, beginning in 1890.

1. *Pg. 538 Chapter* Ⅳ *"The New Revelation" by Arthur Conan Doyle, Kindle Edition.*
2. *Pg. 167 "The Spirits' Book" (New English Edition) by Allan Kardec, Luchnos Media LLC, Kindle Edition.*

House of Ogai Mori and Soseki Natsume, photo: Museum Meiji-Mura

The following is a simple timeline of Natsume Sōseki's life.

1867 Born in Tokyo in January

1890 Entered Imperial University as an English Literature major

1893 Graduated, continued to graduate school

1895 Became a middle school teacher in Matsuyama

1896 Married, left post as teacher

1900 Went abroad to England via the Ministry of Education, Science, and Culture

1903 Returned to Japan
Became a teacher at First Higher School and a professor of humanities at Tokyo Imperial University;
moved to the house at Sendagi in March

1904 Began keeping a cat in early summer

1905 I Am A Cat published in *Hototogisu*

1906 Botchan, Kusamakura published;
left Sendagi house in December

1907 Left teaching posts to join *Asahi Shimbun* in April;
began efforts to be a professional writer

1916 Died of a stomach ulcer in December

Excerpt from *Sōseki* no Omoide («Remembering Sōseki"), by Natsume Kyoko Years have been converted to Western calendar

It seems that the author had already begun suffering from mental instability during his time in England, but after returning to Japan and moving into this house in 1903, his mental condition became unstable in the summer, leading to his living separately from his family from July to September.

According to his wife, from around spring of 1904, his mental condition had stabilized again. At the beginning of summer in that year, the cat became a member of his home. The details of how this came to be are described in the novel, but his wife, who hated cats, would repeatedly try to chase the cat away, only for it to keep coming back. When Sōseki heard that she was thinking of abandoning the cat in some distant location, he yelled at her, asking, "Why can't you just leave it alone?" This appears to have been enough to solidify the cat's place in their home. It was, in this sense, a cat that Sōseki invited into his home himself. Afterwards, a masseuse who visited their home told Sōseki's wife, "Ma'am, this cat, fully black down to the claw, is a rare sort of lucky cat. If you raise it to be big and healthy, it will make your family prosper" (from *Sōseki no Omoide*). After this, she cherished the cat as a member of the family herself. Indeed, the cat proved to bring fortune to the Natsume household. I Am A Cat, which Sōseki wrote as little more than a page-filler for a magazine at a friend's request, garnered wide acclaim and became a bestseller. However, there is one more thing that appears to have contributed to the birth of "Natsume Sōseki, the writer." This is the study that was in that house in Sendagi, which was built around 1887 by a certain businessman.

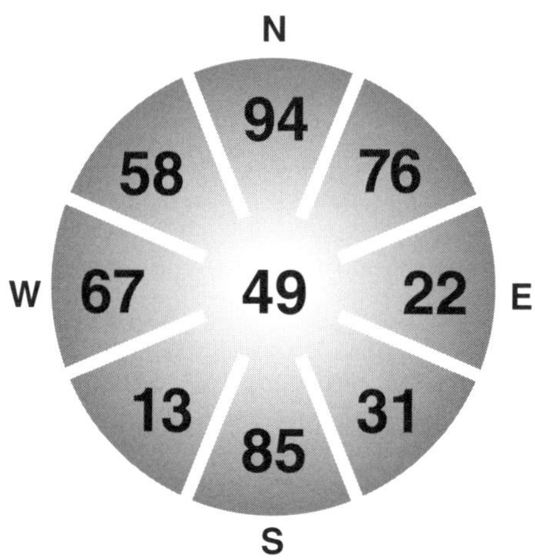

Figure 18: Flying Star Chart: 1887 Completion, Age 2, Facing East 2–3

Numbers on the bearings are as follows:

Left side: Spiritual Star

Right side: Wealth Star

Ex: North bearing: 94; 9 Spiritual Star, 4 Wealth Star

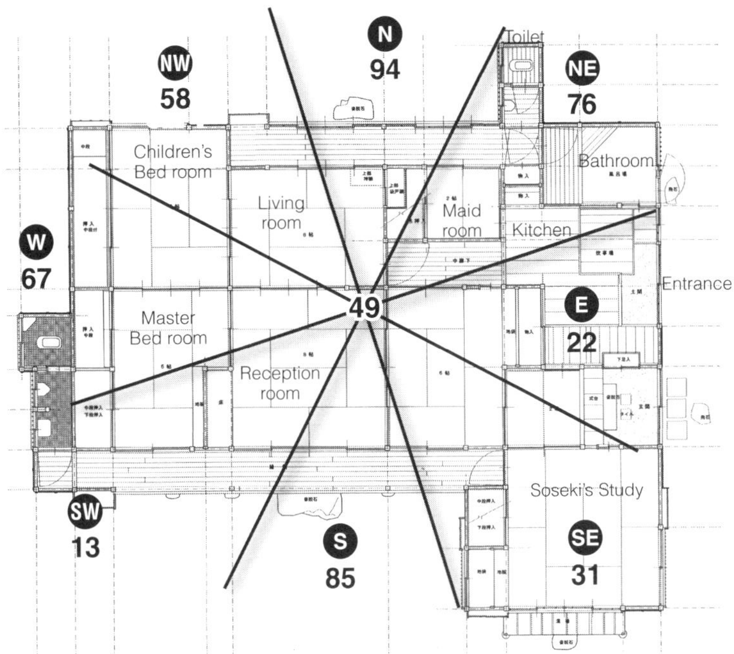

Figure 19: Floor Plan of Sōseki's house, the Museum Meiji-Mura

Sōseki lived in this house from March of 1903 to December of 1906, marking the transition from Age 2 to Age 3. 1903 was the last year of Age 2; as Age 3 energy would have already been quite strong at this point, the analysis will be based on Age 3 flying star energy.

The famed cat entered the Natsume household in the early summer of 1904, the first official year of Age 3. Natsume Sōseki began writing the novel at the end of this year.

Age 3 1904–1023

The most auspicious stars: Wealth Star 3, Spiritual Star 3

The auspicious stars: Wealth Star 4, Spiritual Star 4

As flying stars 5 and 2 are the most inauspicious, flying star 5 does not take the third auspicious star position, leaving only flying stars 3 and 4.

Wealth Star 3 (Southwest)

The strongest Wealth Star is in the southwest bearing. Beyond this bearing is a middle school with a large schoolyard. While Sōseki was known to be irritated by the stray balls that would occasionally come whizzing over, this schoolyard has the effect of activating Wealth Star 3.

Wealth Star 4 (North)

Wealth Star 4, the second-strongest auspicious star, was in the *chanoma* (Japanese-style living room); beyond the garden lived a *koto* instructor whose music was audible from the Natsume house, activating this star as well.

While Sōseki was an educator at this time, he had published in magazines before. However, I Am A Cat is thought to be his first publication which provided him income. According to his wife Kyoko, he started earning manuscript fees, which enabled the family to recover items they had sold at pawn shops. We might surmise that this was thanks to the activation of their financial luck by way of the auspicious Wealth Stars.

Spiritual Star 3 (Southeast)

Sōseki's study was occupied by the strongest Spiritual Star at the time, Spiritual Star 3. Details of Sōseki's study are discussed further below.

Spiritual Star 4 (Center)

As there was neither bedroom nor study in the central bearing, this star's energy was not in use.

Sōseki and his wife's bedroom was a Japanese-style room that spanned the southwest and west bearings, straddling Spiritual Stars 6 and 1. While these were stars in decline, they were not inauspicious for Sōseki, who was Kuan number 7.

The entrance in the east bearing had Wealth Star 2, which was not good for the health of the residents. Sōseki suffered from both physical and mental ailments throughout his life; to borrow a phrase from his wife, Sōseki suffered from "ailments of the mind" while living here, as well, which led to his family staying away from the house for a period. To refer back to the auspicious Spiritual Star in the entrance mentioned in Chapter 2, an Age 2 building established in 1903 had an auspicious Wealth Star 2 in the entrance at the same time as an auspicious Spiritual Star 2 occupying it, which likely led to a bad environment for resident health.

Sōseki and the Study with the Most Auspicious Spiritual Star

Sōseki no Omoide, a collection of writings by Natsume Kyoko, Sōseki's wife, describes Sōseki during his time at this house in detail.

Around the end of this year (1904, author's clarification), for some reason, Sōseki was suddenly filled with motivation to write. He published I Am A Cat in the New Year edition of *Hototogisu*, Tower of London in the New Year edition of *Teikoku Bungaku*, and The Carlyle Museum in *Gakukan*. I don't know much about creative things, but while he hadn't shown any interest in writing novels professionally before, it seems that he had always desperately wanted to write but had held himself back. Once he started writing, he wrote things one after another after another. In the next year, he wrote the rest of "Cat," (...), as well as Botchan and Kusamakura. Not a month went by without him publishing something in a magazine somewhere, but whenever I saw him writing, he seemed to be having so much fun. He'd write, at latest, until midnight or one, but in general, he'd get back from the school and write, seemingly effortlessly, before and after dinner, until around ten. I don't remember how long any particular work took, but I do remember feeling so happy watching the way he could get going on a novel the second he put his pen to the paper. This was well beyond just getting into the swing of the work. He almost never even made an error as he was writing. I'm not sure if he became unable to write in the same way as he got older, or if that happened after writing something difficult, or if he was just unusually possessed during this period. Either way, I don't really understand what was going on with him during that period. It was like he was trying to clear out all the things he needed to write in order to get all his practice out of the way.

From *Sōseki no Omoide*

Botchan was supposedly written in about two weeks.

Sōseki in his study in Sendagi (1906), Photo: Wikimedia Commons

In December of 1906, the owner of the house returned to Tokyo, and the Natsume family had to move out. Four months later, in April of 1907, Sōseki joined Asahi Shimbun as an in-house literary writer, ending his career as an educator and becoming a full-time writer.

According to "My Father, Natsume Sōseki," written by Sōseki's son, Natsume Shinroku, Sōseki had originally planned to become an architect when he was young.

Afterwards, he apparently said, "I'm not very proactive in anything I do, so I'm surprised myself. I became a writer at the suggestion of a friend, I even became an educator because a friend suggested it to me... it seems that everyone who writes novels is like this. In that sense, you could say that I am the invention of other people."

After its initial publication in Hototogisu–whose chief editor was the friend who pushed Sōseki to submit a manuscript – I Am A Cat was an instant hit, was serialized, and eventually became a bestseller.

We might say that it was a combination of innate talent, an encounter with a lucky cat, and a special study in a house in Sendagi that brought about the Natsume Sōseki we remember today.

Master Bedroom and Study in the House Where Hemingway Wrote 70% of All of His Works

Natsume Sōseki lived in the house above during Age 3. Next let's look at an author who lived in a house during Age 4. We'll discuss the house of Ernest Hemingway, located in Key West, Florida, USA.

In Natsume Sōseki's house, the study during his time was occupied by the most auspicious star, but in the Key West house, both the bedroom and the desk in the study were activated by the most auspicious star. They also share a common point in the lucky cats that they raised. While Sōseki's cat was completely black, Hemingway's cat had six toes on its front paws, which he believed, as they say, made the cat lucky. Sōseki did not have any special fondness for cats in general, but Hemingway was a cat lover, and the descendants of this cat continue to live and be lovingly protected at the Hemingway house.

A cat that came to say hello | Photos by the author, 2018

The following is a simple timeline of Ernest Hemingway's life.

1899 Born in Oak Park, Illinois, USA in July

1917 Joined the most influential newspaper company of the time as a journalist apprentice

1918 Quit the newspaper company to become a Red Cross driver on the Italian Front; while in Europe, was seriously injured from artillery fire.

1921 Married Hadley Richardson

1923 Decided to become an author

1926 Published The Sun Also Rises

1927 Divorced Hadley and married Pauline Pfeiffer, a journalist at Vogue

1928 Visited Key West for the first time

1929 Published A Farewell to Arms

1931 Moved into the now—"Hemingway House" on Whitehead Street in Key West in December

1932 Published Death in the Afternoon

1933 Published the short story anthology, Winner Take Nothing; began submitting articles to the newly-founded Esquire Magazine (a total of 17, until 1936)

1935 Published Green Hills of Africa

1936 Published The Snows of Kilimanjaro and The Short Happy Life of Francis Macomber

1937 Published To Have and Have Not

1938 Published Old Man at the Bridge and The Fifth Column and the First Forty-Nine Stories

1939 Began For Whom the Bell Tolls; **left the Key West house in December**

1940 Divorced Pauline; published For Whom the Bell Tolls
Held a wedding ceremony with Martha Ellis Gellhorn in America; purchased Finca Vigia, his house in Havana, Cuba

1945 Divorced Martha.

1946 Married Mary Welsh, his final wife.

1952 Published The Old Man and the Sea

1953 Received the Pulitzer Prize for The Old Man and the Sea

1954 Received serious injuries after two consecutive plane crashes in Africa, which left him in ill health for the rest of his life. Receives the Nobel Prize in Literature.

1961 Committed suicide by shotgun

Since being gravely wounded from artillery fire in Europe at the age of 19, Hemingway lived a life full of serious injuries and poor health while jet-setting around the globe like a migratory fish.

Even while living in Key West, Hemingway never stayed in one place for very long, moving through Havana, Africa, Paris, New York, and Madrid.

When he met the Vogue reporter, Pauline Pfeiffer, in Paris, he was still married to Hadley Richardson. In 1927, he divorced Hadley to marry Pauline.

The following year, they visited Key West at the suggestion of a friend, and continued to visit thereafter. Pauline wanted to live in Paris, but because Hemingway was taken with Key West, they found a way to compromise their desires and move into a house on Whitehead Street which was, at that time, in dilapidated condition. It was given to them in 1931 as a wedding present from Pauline's uncle; at this time, the Great Depression had just begun, and there were many vacant properties in Florida.

The house was built in 1851, and at the time Hemingway received it, it was in a ruinous state with holes in the ceiling and almost all of the windows broken. Pauline conducted renovation work and imported furniture from France and Spain, making it habitable in two months.

Hemingway was particularly drawn to a small two-story shed at the back of the house. In the past, the first floor of the shed was used as a carriage house, while the servant that tended to it lived in the room above. It was connected to the main building by a long, narrow kitchen.

Hemingway turned the second floor of the shed into a study, while creating a passageway along the roof of the old kitchen that enabled him to access it directly from the bedroom on the second floor. Every day after eating breakfast in the bedroom, he would access this catwalk from the balcony to get to his study. In 1948, the catwalk and old kitchen both were destroyed by a hurricane, and were never rebuilt.

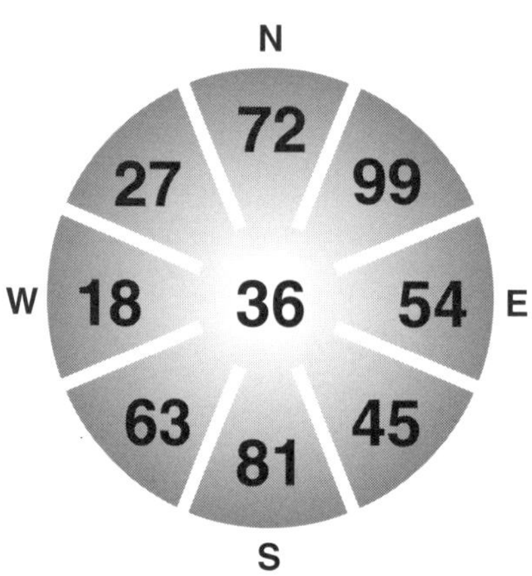

Figure 20: Flying Star Chart: 1851 Construction, Age 2, Facing Southwest2–3

Numbers on the bearings are as follows:
Left side: Spiritual Star
Right side: Wealth Star
Ex: North bearing: 72; 7 Spiritual Star, 2 Wealth Star

Hemingway lived in this house from 1931–1939, corresponding to Age 4.

Age 4 | 1924–1943
The most auspicious stars: Wealth Star 4, Spiritual Star 4
The auspicious stars: Wealth Star 5, Spiritual Star 5
The little auspicious stars: Wealth Star 6, Spiritual Star 6

As there is no bedroom or study on the first floor, only the Wealth Star energies are at play.

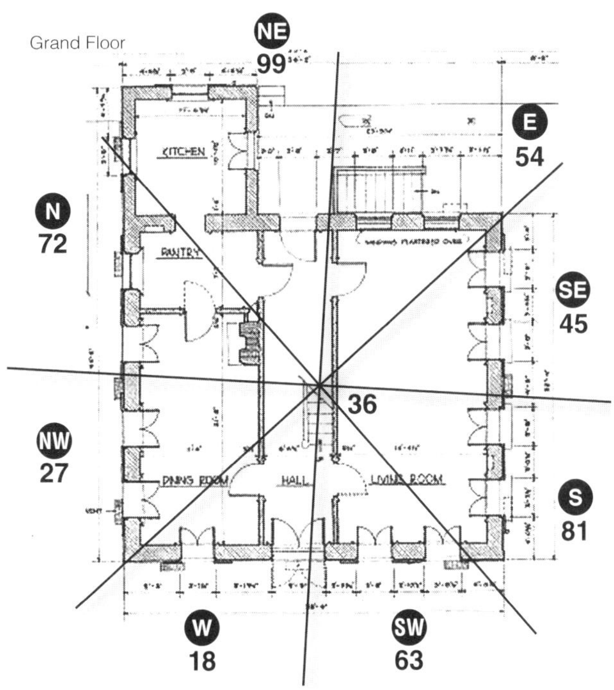

Figure 21: Hemingway House, Ground Floor floorplan

Wealth Star 4 (East), Wealth Star 5 (South East)

The two most auspicious stars are in the living room, and as the room faces the garden, it is further activated.

Wealth Star 1 (South)

Part of the living room. This is a weak star, but its inauspicious effect is not very strong (Flying Star 1, 4, 6, 8, 9 are not so harmful when their energies are declining).

Wealth Star 3 (Southwest)

Part of the living room. This star's energy has a tendency to cause arguments.

Wealth Star 8 (West)

Front entrance. This is an inauspicious star until the end of Age 5 and has an energy that tends to cause misfortune for young boys, but like flying stars 1, 4, 6, and 9, the misfortune is not that strong.

Wealth Star 7 (Northwest)

Dining room. While the star here will become mildly auspicious in Age 5, when Hemingway lived here in Age 4, it was an inauspicious star. During this Age, it can cause legal troubles and careless remarks.

Wealth Star 2 (North)

Pantry. This is an inauspicious star, but has no effect on this room. Wealth Star in a storage area or in a pantry can't be active.

Wealth Star 9 (Northeast)

Kitchen. This is an inauspicious star until Age 7. The energy of this star can be particularly dangerous for women.

Wealth Star 6 (Center)

Staircase. While the energy of this star is still weak in Age 4, it is activated because of its presence in a staircase.

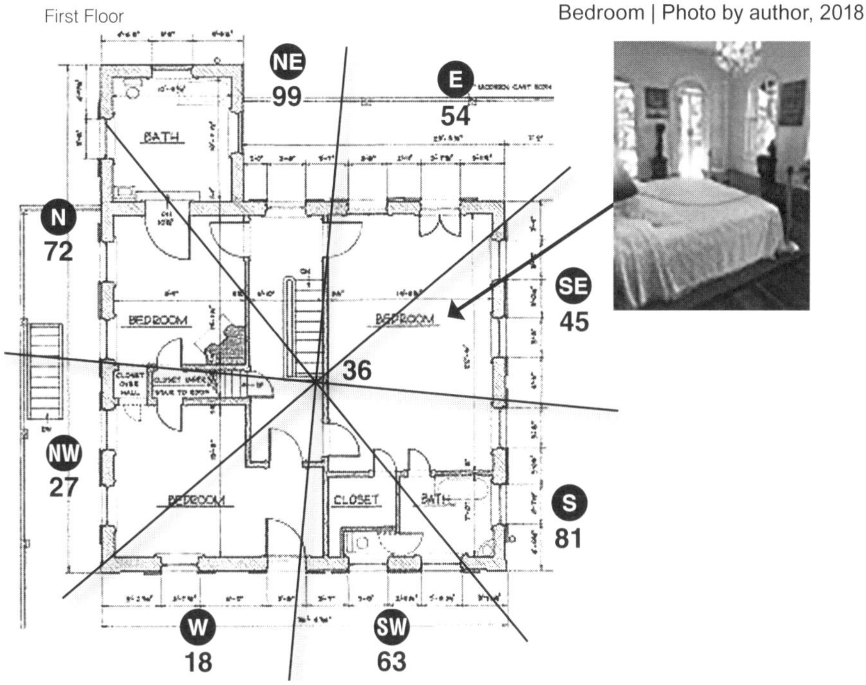

Figure 22: Hemingway House, second floor floorplan

As for the first floor, I will only evaluate the Spiritual Stars in the bedroom.

Spiritual Star 5 (East), Spiritual Star 4 (Southeast)

In Hemingway's time, the most auspicious spiritual star, Spiritual Star 4 (southeast), and auspicious spiritual star, Spiritual Star 5 (east), were present where Hemingway's bed was located in his bedroom. For the time, it was a most fortunate location for a bedroom.

Spiritual Star 2 (Northwest)

Using this bearing for a bedroom or a study during this Age results in undesirable energy, not good for the health.

Spiritual Star 7 (North)

This was an inauspicious star during Hemingway's Age 4 residence, but became a lesser auspicious star in Age 5.

As can be seen in this house, when an auspicious Wealth Star and auspicious Spiritual Star are in the same bearing in a two-story building, it is ideal to have areas on the ground floor like the entrance and living room be activated by the Wealth Stars, while bedrooms and studies on the first floor are activated by Spiritual Stars. While the entrance of the house was visited by the inauspicious Wealth Star 8 during Hemingway's time in the house, the activity of the Wealth Star in the living room, facing a garden, likely overcame any problems for financial fortune that the inauspicious star could have caused.

Writing studio | Photo by the author, 2018

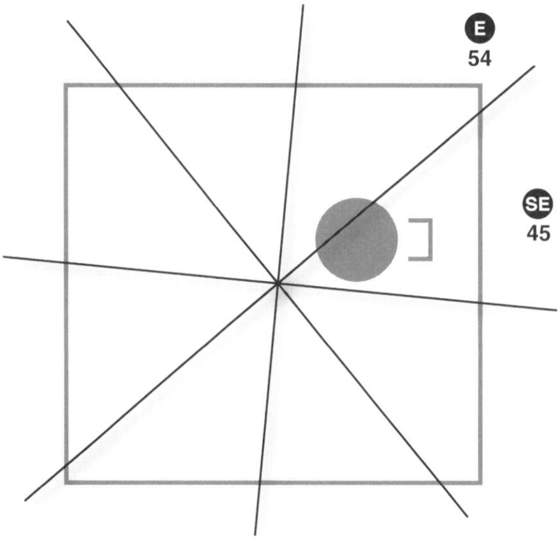

Figure 23: Floorplan of Hemingway's study and desk, with its Flying Stars

Currently, the shed is completely independent from the main building, facing a pool to the southeast. However, when Hemingway lived in this house, the shed was connected to the building, and as such, the isolated study was still part of the chart of the main building. Assuming that Hemingway's desk at the house museum is in the same location that it was when Hemingway lived there, it perfectly overlaps both the Spiritual Star 4 and Spiritual Star 5 bearings. That is to say, Hemingway both slept in a bedroom graced by an auspicious Spiritual Star and wrote at a desk graced by Spiritual Stars.

About five years after Hemingway moved into the house, in December of 1936, Hemingway met a charming woman who had come to Key West with intention to meet him, at one of his favorite haunts: Sloppy Joe's Bar. This woman introduced herself to Hemingway as a journalist named Martha Gellhorn. The spark was undeniable. The war journalist side of Hemingway was rekindled, and he joined Martha to work as a war correspondent in the Spanish Civil War that had recently broken out.

At the same time, there were plans to create a pool in the garden of the house, and work on it had commenced. While Hemingway conducted his reporting work on the Spanish Civil War from 1937 to 1938, he had Pauline continue the pool construction. The pool used a well to pump saltwater for filling and the expense is said to have been extravagant. When Hemingway returned from his reporting trip, he was astonished at the final cost. He said that he'll pay the final penny, and in commemoration, buried the coin alongside the pool.

The Pool That May Have Weakened the Auspicious Spiritual Star

On the topic of the pool, its location lay right across the line of the east and southeast bearing of the bedroom, which may have led to activation of Wealth Stars 4 and 5. Of course, activating auspicious Wealth Stars is good for financial fortune, but it may have resulted in the weakening of Spiritual Stars 4 and 5. The pool was in direct sight of the study, such that Spiritual Star 4 may have been weakened in the study as well. This may have resulted in negative influence on harmonious relationships and inspiration.

The pool was completed in 1938, but beginning in the preceding year, Pauline became aware of the relationship between Martha and her husband, which led to an increasing frequency in arguments. In spite of repeated efforts to rehabilitate their relationship, all unsuccessful, in December of 1939, Hemingway packed up his belongings and left the Key West house. The couple divorced in the following year, and Hemingway purchased a house in Cuba for him and Martha. Until her sudden death in 1951, Pauline was left alone to care for their son in the Key West house.

Pool |
Photo by the author, 2018

This may have happened regardless of if the pool was constructed or not.

It seems that Hemingway was unsatisfied with his peaceful life of writing and fishing, and in reality, Martha was in the same position that Pauline was once in with Hemingway's first wife. However, if the completion of the pool could be thought of as one of the couple's attempts to mend their relationship, from the perspective of Flying Star Feng Shui, it was doomed to failure.

The Final House of Marilyn Monroe

We've now looked at authors who lived in houses activated by auspicious Spiritual Stars in Age 3 and Age 4, respectively. Now let's look at a house inhabited by a certain celebrity in Age 5.

In August of 1962, the legendary American actress, Marilyn Monroe, was found dead in the bedroom of her home by her housekeeper. Monroe had barely been living in the house for half a year.

Monroe's death has been variously described as a suicide, a murder, or accidental; the real story remains unclear. What follows is a brief timeline of her life.

1926 Born in Los Angeles, USA, to a single mother. As her mother was unable to support her, she spent her childhood in foster homes and orphanages

1942 Married James Dougherty, an airline mechanic

1944 Became an in-house model for a modeling agency

1946 Marriage ended in divorce. Signed a one-year contract with 20th Century Fox: the birth of «Marilyn Monroe"

1954 Married Joe DiMaggio. Increasing popularity, despite a marriage headed for disaster. Received first psychological assessment.

1956 Divorced Joe DiMaggio, married Arthur Miller.

1962 Divorced Arthur Miller, was institutionalized, and began receiving psychiatric treatment. Moved into the house at Brentwood in March. Found dead in her home on August 5th.[3]

According to the English journalist Anthony Summers' Goddess: The Secret Lives of Marilyn Monroe, the psychiatrist that examined Monroe, Dr. Greenson, encouraged her to buy the house.

3 *Summers, Anthony. Goddess: The Secret Lives of Marilyn Monroe (P.353-354). Orion. Kindle Edition.*

Quote[4]**:**

As 1962 began, at Dr. Greenson's suggestion, Marilyn began to look for a house of her own. She had never owned her own home, and Greenson hoped it would give her security, and encourage her to stop thinking of herself as a homeless orphan. Marilyn began house-hunting, helped by Eunice Murray, a sixty-year-old woman with some experience in looking after psychiatric patients...

At the end of January, though, a house was found—a modest, single-story home in the residential district of Brentwood. The style was Mexican, like Dr. Greenson's house, with wood beamed ceilings, a large, central living area, and small bedrooms. The house was a far cry from the ostentatious homes expected of Hollywood stars, but it was what Marilyn wanted. It was at the closed end of a cul-de-sac, and therefore private...

Marilyn burst into tears when she signed the contract for the Brentwood house, and explained later, 'I felt badly because I was buying a home all alone.' By early 1962, Dr. Greenson felt the drug problem was under control, and hoped Marilyn was at last going to make real progress. Nobody, it seems, took note of the odd little coat of arms emblazoned on tiles outside the front door of the house. The motto read, in Latin, Cursum Perficio. This means, in English, 'I am finishing my journey.' Marilyn was nearly thirty-six. She had six months to live. *(Abridged text)*

Perhaps the one who built this house intended it as a final abode.

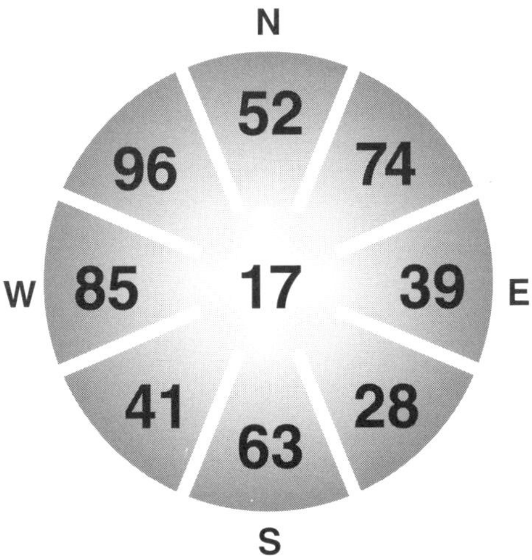

Figure 24: Flying Star Chart: 1929 Construction, Age 4, Facing Northeast 2–3

4. *Summers, Anthony. Goddess: The Secret Lives of Marilyn Monroe (P.353-354). Orion. Kindle Edition.*

Numbers on the bearings are as follows:

Left side: Spiritual Star

Right side: Wealth Star

Example: North bearing: Spiritual 5, Wealth Star 2

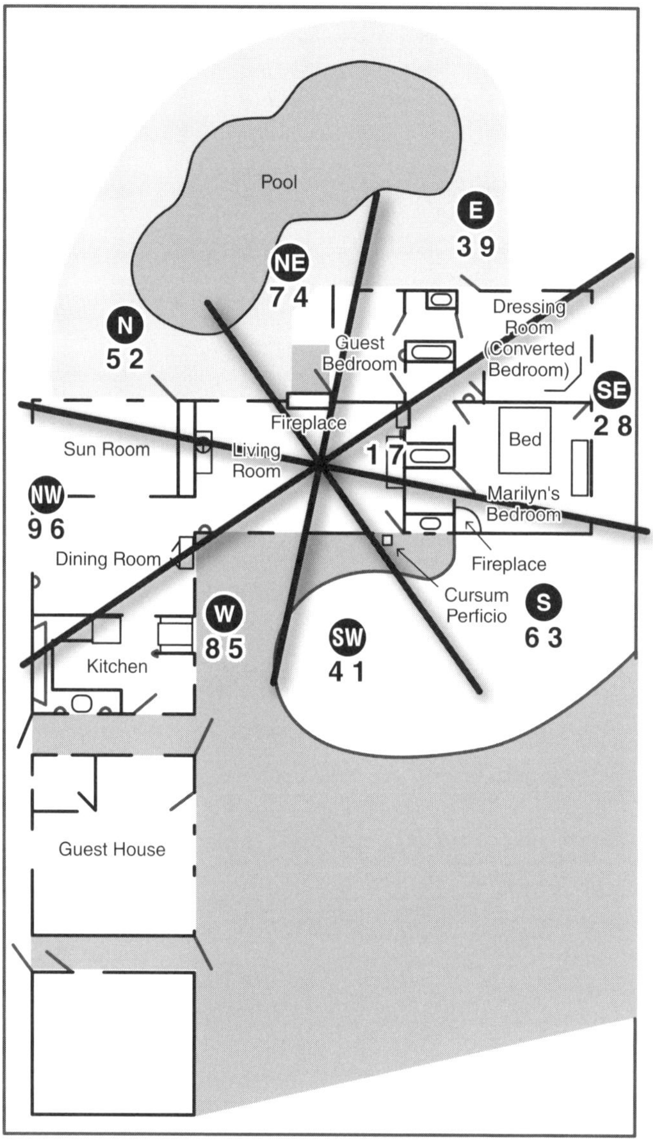

Figure 25: Final house of Marilyn Monroe, floorplan with Flying Stars

Monroe lived in this house in 1962, nearing the end of Age 5, two years from the start of Age 6.

Age 5 1944–1963

The major auspicious stars: Wealth Star 5, Spiritual Star 5
The auspicious stars: Wealth Star 6, Spiritual Star 6
The minor auspicious stars: Wealth Star 7, Spiritual Star 7

Monroe's house was a Mexican-style mansion in Brentwood, a quiet suburb of Los Angeles. Based on this property's Flying Star chart, it was ill-advised at the time to recommend it to someone like Monroe who suffered from health and privacy issues.

Auspicious Stars

Wealth Star 5 (West)

This star is in the kitchen, but as the outside entrance is adjacent to the guest house, it is not particularly active.

Wealth Star 6 (Northwest)

This star flies through the sunroom and dining room. Since Age 6 was soon to come, at the time, this star likely had a fair amount of influence. While there are windows, it does not face the pool–which strongly activates Wealth Stars–limiting its energy.

Wealth Star 7 (Center)

Being in the center, this star cannot move about freely, so despite being auspicious, its effects are likely to be limited.

Spiritual Star 5 (North)

As this star is in the sunroom and faces the pool, its energy is very weak.

Spiritual Star 6 (South)

As this star is in the entrance, there is the possibility of it causing problems in health and relationships for residents (refer to the discussion of auspicious Spiritual Stars in entrances in Chapter 2)

Spiritual Star 7 (Northeast)

As this star is in the living room, its energy is weak.

Inauspicious Stars

Bedroom: Spiritual Star 2 (Southeast), a bringer of illness

Wealth and Spiritual Stars 4 and 5 are very inauspicious in Ages other than 4 or 5, but in Age 5, they are very auspicious. In Age 5, the most inauspicious stars are Spiritual Star 2 and Wealth Star 2. Spiritual Star 2 was present in Monroe's bedroom. The energy of Spiritual Star 2 is especially detrimental to health.

In an interview with Richard Meryman for Life magazine just before her death, she mentioned her difficulty sleeping. Of course, Monroe's instability preceded her moving into this house, so it is likely that this was not entirely the fault of the inauspicious Spiritual Star in her bedroom.

Entrance: Wealth Star 3 (South), a bringer of conflict and burglary

This is the entrance that had the aforementioned Latin phrase emblazoned on a plate. This entrance has Wealth Star 3, which in this Age exerted an energy that can invite conflict and violation.

Along with the presence of auspicious Spiritual Star 6, this was an unlucky entrance indeed (refer to the discussion of auspicious Spiritual Stars in entrances in Chapter 2).

The residents who moved in afterwards, Veronica Hamel and her husband, are said to have found surveillance cameras and listening devices in the ceilings and walls in the process of renovating the house.[5]

While Monroe's cause of death has been proposed as suicide, murder, or accident, there remains no conclusive story. It is difficult to use a feng shui chart to determine the true cause of death, but from the perspective of feng shui, in consideration of Marilyn Monroe's health conditions and private issues at the time of her moving into this house, it would not be surprising if one of these theories were true.

— The most inauspicious Spiritual Star at the time was in the bedroom

— The bringer of illness, Wealth Star 2, was facing the pool

---

5. *https://www.thespruce.com/marilyn-monroes-los-angeles-house-4063952*

— The auspicious Spiritual Star (Spiritual Star 5) was on a door (north bearing) facing the entrance and pool
— All of the Wealth Stars in the entrance facing the pool were inauspicious

However, it must be stressed that for someone who was sound in body and mind, had relatively good luck, and didn't have the same kinds of personal problems that Monroe had would not likely have faced a similar tragic outcome had they moved into this house at this time. At most, the issues would be restricted to things like having difficulty falling asleep, or not having restful, or other inconveniences of this nature. However, if one were to live in such a place for a long time, the vicissitudes of life may be compounded in an unfortunate way. Once a new residence has been chosen, it is advisable to make adjustments in accordance with the principles of feng shui that are suitable for the Age.

Renovation Recommendations for Living in This House in Age 9 (2024–2043)

I'd like to suggest some renovations for living in the Monroe house in Age 9. In terms of financial fortune, this 20-year period, until 2043, is guided by the most auspicious Wealth Star 9 and Spiritual Star 9 and the auspicious Wealth Star 1 and Spiritual Star 1.

— Wealth Star 9 is in the entrance that faces the pool. Since the eastern guest bedroom will be activated by this Wealth Star, it should be turned into a dining room.
— While this is a living room, the fireplace counteracts Wealth Star 4, so it is fine as it is.
— If the entrance in Wealth Star 3's bearing is moved to the southwest bearing with Wealth Star 1 which is auspicious, wealth luck will be activated until 2063.
— The kitchen extends across the southeast and south bearings; as a stovetop is a measure against Wealth Star 3, it should be placed in the south bearing.
— The bedroom should be moved to the northwest bearing, where the most auspicious Spiritual Star 9 is active. All that is necessary is that one's head is in the Spiritual Star 9 bearing, it should be possible for two rooms to make use of its energy. Since the other auspicious spiritual star, Spiritual Star 1, is in the center where a living room is, it is unusable.
— It is advisable to turn the kitchen area in the west bearing that holds inauspicious Wealth Star 5 into a bathroom.

Suggestions for Work from Home

The onset of the COVID-19 pandemic in 2020 resulted in dramatic changes in work and lifestyles around the world. As the opportunity to work from home increased, the importance of residential feng shui increased as well. Until this point, commuting to an office enabled financial fortune to be focused on stores and offices, while residences could focus more on health and relationships. Once homes became synonymous with offices, there arose the need to consider these buildings in terms of these dual functions.

In order to improve financial fortune, it is important to focus on ensuring that Wealth Stars are present in locations such as entrances, living rooms, areas with windows, staircases, and atriums. For health and inspiration, the focus must be on Spiritual Stars in bedrooms and places for work. If we assume that working from home requires a laptop or computer, it is ideal for a Wealth Star to be active in the home office or wherever the computer is used. This is because Wealth Stars are more powerful in areas with electronic appliances than Spiritual Stars are. Ideally, a home office might be established in a corner of a bearing that has a living room visited by an auspicious Wealth Star.

On the other hand, if the computer is not being used for conferences or meetings and there is no TV or background music, a very nice home office can be set up in a bearing with an auspicious Spiritual Star. This choice would be most suitable for work that involves writing, drafting, planning, or making art. It would be, if you will, a room that is suited for meditation.

In Age 9, there are only two auspicious Wealth and Spiritual Stars. If Wealth Star 9 or 1 is in the entrance, living room, or staircase, and Spiritual Star 9 or 1 is where one's desk or bedroom is located, the home should be suitable for working from home during Age 9.

Works Cited

On Natsume Sōseki

Sōseki no Omoide, an anthology by Natsume Kyoko, Bungeibunshu Press

My Father, Natsume Sōseki, by Natsume Shinroku, Bungeibunshu Press

Photo: *Museum Meiji-Mura Wikimedia Commons*

On Hemingway

Biography

Hemingway's Cats and His Women, by Imamura Tateo, CITY BOOKS

Papa Hemingway in Key West by James McLendon The Ketch & Yawl Press

https://www.hemingwayhome.com/

Map

https://www.openstreetmap.org/?mlat=24.55119&mlon=-81.80062&zoom=15#map=19/24.55120/-81.80057

Photo

1 Pixabay License

On Marilyn Monroe

(1) https://www.pexels.com/ja-jp/photo/53453/

(2) Biography

Maririn Monroo no Shinjitsu, by Anthony Summers (translation), Fusosha Publishing

(3) Goddess: The Secret Lives of Marilyn Monroe (P.353–354) by Anthony Summers. Orion. Kindle edition.

(4)https://themarilynmonroecollection.com/cursum-perficio-the-series-part-ii-the-inside-of-the-house/

(5) https://www.thespruce.com/marilyn-monroes-los-angeles-house-4063952

(6)https://www.thespruce.com/thmb/jhjlejmmb7hRfyAcC5PUGIo1hBI=/960x0/filters:no_upscale():max_bytes(150000):strip_icc()/GettyImages-1180111-58db5dc53df78c5162a8a299.jpg

Chapter 8

The Foundations of Ancient Chinese Science

This book, as a whole, is primarily aimed at individuals who do not have access to feng shui professionals, but who are nonetheless interested in using feng shui techniques in their own homes and businesses. As such, most of the theory behind feng shui has been ignored in prior chapters, in favor of more accessible explanations. This chapter is intended for readers who want to understand Flying Star feng shui in greater detail. Here, the foundations of Flying Star feng shui are described in terms of their origin in ancient Chinese scientific practice.

Yin and Yang

The ancient Chinese made sense of creation in terms of the emergence, from nothingness, of a balance between "yin," a void, submissive, reductive, or dark force, and "yang," a present, assertive, adductive, or bright force. The origin of the universe itself lies in the appearance of this duality from a state of absolute absence.

The abstract duality of yin and yang encompasses binary contrasts such as male and female, sun and moon, good and evil, light and darkness, beauty and ugliness. The very concept of "good" necessitates a concept of "evil" for comparison. Without these contrasts, it is not possible to establish meaning.

The following figure displays the Tai chi, which symbolizes the interaction and symbiosis of yin and yang.

Tai chi

White represents yang, while black represents yin. Yang increases in strength little by little from the bottom, and when it reaches its maximum strength, it creates yin–the black dot inside the white. At the same time, when yin is at its strongest, yang emerges. The black dot inside the white and the white dot inside the black represent the inherent relation between these two extremes: they cannot exist without each other, and each one creates the other.

8 Trigrams

The scholars of ancient China described yin and yang as the forces that created the universe, but they described these forces in terms of two different types of lines.

Yang is represented by an unbroken line, whereas yin is represented by a broken line (two line segments). These two different types of lines were combined into groups of three (trigrams) to represent natural phenomena and the seasons. Given two types of lines, in groups of three, there are 2 × 2 × 2 = 8 combinations, or 8 trigrams.

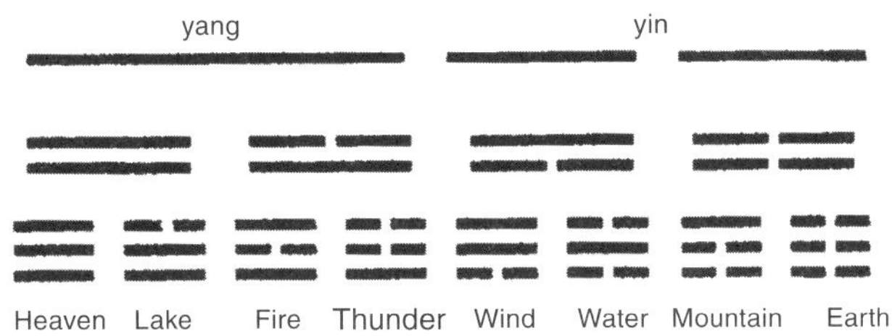

Figure 26: The Eight Trigram System

8 Trigrams Early Arrangement (showing natural phenomena, topography)

The eight-trigram chart structure below was, according to legend, originally devised in 4500 BC by the mythical king Fu Hsi. Charts such as these are thought to be combination maps of both local topography or natural phenomena.

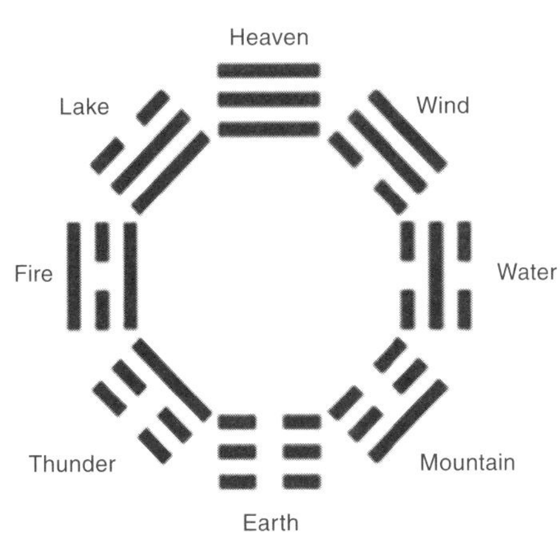

Figure 27: 8 Trigrams Early Arrangement

Reference material

"Theory of Natural Phenomena" (from "The Numerology of the I Ching" by Grand Master Alfred Huang [1])

He found that wherever he went, heaven was always there above him and so hung the symbol of Heaven at the top. (On ancient Chinese maps, south always appears on top.) Because he found that wherever he stepped, earth was always there below him, he hung the symbol of Earth at the bottom.

Between Heaven and Earth there were two objects that attracted him the most: the sun and the moon. He hung the symbol of the sun in the east and the symbol of the moon in the west. Because the sun is the source of heat and light he decided that its symbol also represented Fire. The moon however, does not radiate heat and light, so he attributed to it the symbol of Water, because water is cold and its attribute is opposite to that of fore.

There still two other things that drew Fu Xi's attention: the thunder-storm and the wind, which, he realized, have tremendous energy. When the wind was not harsh and the thunder-storm was on time, they were favorable to the crops; they always worked together in close relationship with people's lives. He hung the symbol of Thunder in the northeast and the symbol of Wind in the southwest.

Finally, he hung the symbol of Mountain in the northwest and the symbol of Lake in the southeast, the ancient Chinese associated activating energy with the mountain and soothing energy with the lake.

"Topographic Theory" (from "Feng Shui Essentials" by Grand Master Raymond Lo [2])

The 8 Trigrams are placed in a special order with Heaven on top, in the South, and Earth underneath in the North. To the East is Fire to Symbolize the sun and to the west is Water, the moon, or the opposite to Fire. Then he proceeded to place Trigram in the four corners, in accordance to the geographical setting of China. In the Chinese landscape, the tall mountains are in the Northwest which slope down towards Southeast. Hence, he placed Mountain Trigram in the Northwest and Lake Trigram in the Southeast. In the remaining corners of Southwest and Northeast, he placed the Trigrams Wind for Southwest and Trigram Earthquake for Northeast as Southwest of China has a lot of desserts and no shelter against wind, and Northeast of China is Japan, an earthquake zone.

---

1. *P. 12 "The Numerology of the I Ching" by Alfred Huang*
2. *46 "Feng Shui Essentials" by Raymond Lo*

8 Trigram Later Arrangement (showing seasonal changes)

The following eight-trigram map is said to have been devised by King Wen of the Chau dynasty in B.C.1000. It is thought to incorporate changes in season.

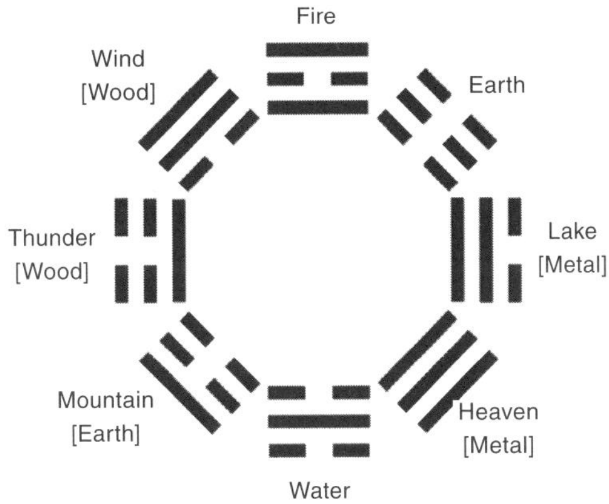

Figure 28: 8 Trigrams Later Arrangement

Reference material

(from "Feng Shui Essentials" by Grand Master Raymond Lo)

He placed Thunder and Wind in East and Southeast, as these two trigrams are wood elements representing Spring season. Then he placed Fire in the south to symbolize summer. He placed the metal trigrams-Lake and Heaven in west and northwest to represent autumn, and Water in the north to represent winter. The earth trigrams Earth and Mountain, is placed on a straight-line opposite to each other in the Southwest and Northeast. This is the center of the Taichi reflecting Earth is important all the year round.

P. 47 "Feng Shui Essentials" by Raymond Lo

The Five Elements: The Forces that Give Rise to All Things

After the duality of yin and yang gave rise to the universe, the five elements populated it with all things.

Reference material

The five elements are wood, fire, earth, metal, and water; their interactions have both constructive and destructive effects. While it is unclear how the five element paradigm arose, it is thought that the system emerged on the east side of the Yellow River in China, before the eight trigrams.

P.25 "The Numerology of the I Ching" by Alfred Huang

The Meaning of the Five Elements

Each of the Five Elements have certain meanings, as described below.

Elements	Metal	Wood	Water	Fire	Earth
Emotion	Grief	Anger	Fear	Joy	Meditation
Internal Organs	Lung	Liver	Kidney	Heart	Stomach
Color	White	Blue Green	Black	Fire	Yellow
Season	Autumn	Spring	Winter	Summer	Four Seasons
Directions	West	East	North	South	Center
Taste	Pungent	Sour	Salty	Bitter	Sweet

Figure 29: The Meaning of the Five Elements

Overview of Trigrams and Elements

The numbers of 8 Trigrams are also Flying Star numbers.

Consequently, the elements of each Flying Star are as follows.

Flying Star 1 → Water

Flying Star 2, 5, 8 → Earth

Flying Star 3, 4 → Wood

Flying Star 6, 7 → Metal

Flying Star 9 → Fire

Reference material

Integration of 8 Trigrams, the Five Elements, the Directions, etc.

(from "The Numerology of the I Ching" by Grand Master Alfred Huang[3])

The concept of the Five Elements was popular during the period of Warring States (475–221 B.C.). At the very beginning, its principle was simple and plain. Before the Han Dynasty (206 B.C.–A.D. 220), the I Ching had no connection with the system of the Five Elements. It was in the Han dynasty that scholars of the Symbol and Number School began to integrate the Eight Primary Gua (8 Trigrams) with yin and yang, the five elements, eight directions, four seasons, the day and the months, and the parts of the human body, and applied them to medicine, the calendar, astrology, and astronomy.

---

3. *P.25 "The Numerology of the I Ching" by Alfred Huang, Inner Traditions, Rochester, Vermont*

Constructive and Destructive relationships of the five elements

The five elements have constructive and destructive relationships as the following image shows.

Wood gives birth to **Fire**

Fire gives birth to **Earth**

Earth gives birth to **Metal**

Metal gives birth to **Water**

Water gives birth to **Wood**

Wood destroys **Earth**

Earth destroys **Water**

Metal destroys **Wood**

Fire destroys **Metal**

Water destroys **Fire**

These relationships are shown in the figure below.

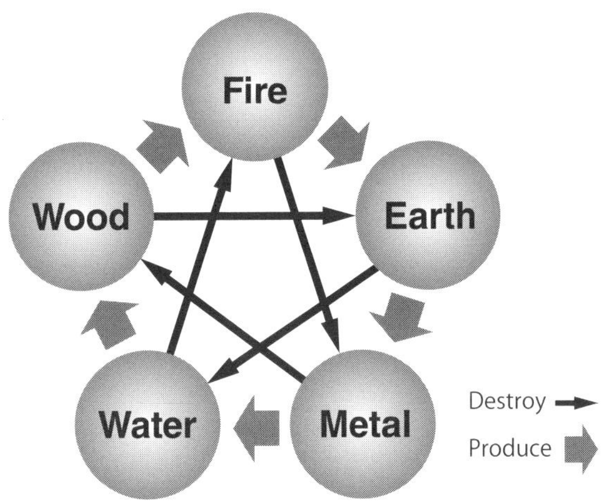

Figure 30: 5 Elements, Cycle of Birth and Cycle of Destruction

Here are some Flying Star feng shui techniques to deal with this sort of energetic activity:

In order to strengthen the element of an auspicious star,
use the same element,
use the element that gives birth to its element, or
use the element that destroys its element.

Similarly, in order to weaken an inauspicious star,
use the element that its element gives birth to, or
use the element that its element destroys.

To give a specific example, in Age 9, the most auspicious stars are Wealth Stars 9 and 1 and Spiritual Stars 9 and 1. Taking Spiritual Star 9 as an example, strengthening Fire requires use of Fire element, Wood element, or Water element.

Similarly, the inauspicious Wealth and Spiritual Stars 5 can be weakened by using the Metal element, which Earth gives birth to, or the Water element, which Earth destroys.

Kua Number and Spiritual Star of the Bedroom

The Kua Number system for choosing bedrooms, described in Chapter 2, is based on the laws of the Five Elements.

Just like the Flying Stars, the Kua Numbers also have respective Elements that define them.

Kua Number	Element
1	Water
2	Earth
3	Wood
4	Wood
6	Metal
7	Metal
8	Earth
9	Fire

If the element of a Spiritual Star in a bedroom has a destructive effect on the element of a person's Kua Number, that bedroom will be bad for their health.

For example, Kua Number 3 has the element of Wood, so people with that Kua Number should avoid bedrooms visited by Spiritual Stars 6 and 7, as these have the Metal element, which destroys Wood.

However, in Age 9, bedrooms with Spiritual Stars 9 and 1 are safe for everyone.

The Lo Shu Diagram and Hoto Numbers

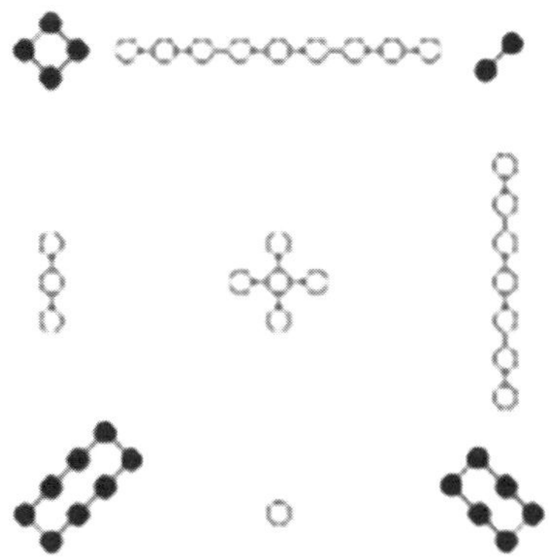

The Lo Shu Diagram

Lo Shu diagram was discovered on the back of a giant tortoise in the River Lo, in around Hsia Dynasty (about 2000 BC).

Figure 31 demonstrates this visually.

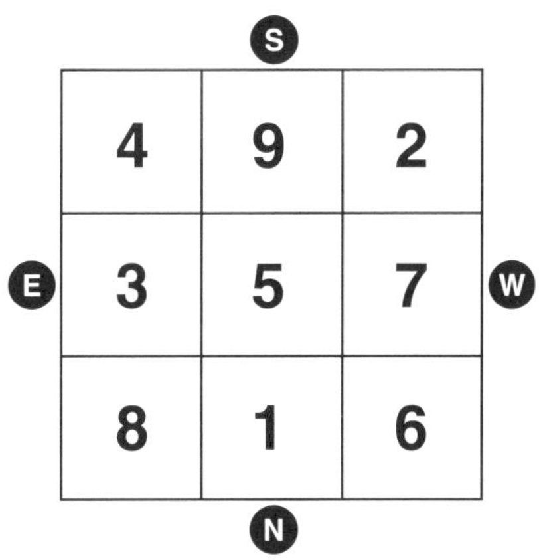

Figure 31: Lo Shu number of arrangement

This figure is also called the Magic Battle Formation. Numbers in every column and row add up to 15. It is said that this configuration is the most efficient distribution for protecting a central area with a limited number of soldiers, and for this reason, was actually used in times of war in Chinese history.

The 8 Trigrams Later Arrangement works in concert with Lo Shu numbers.

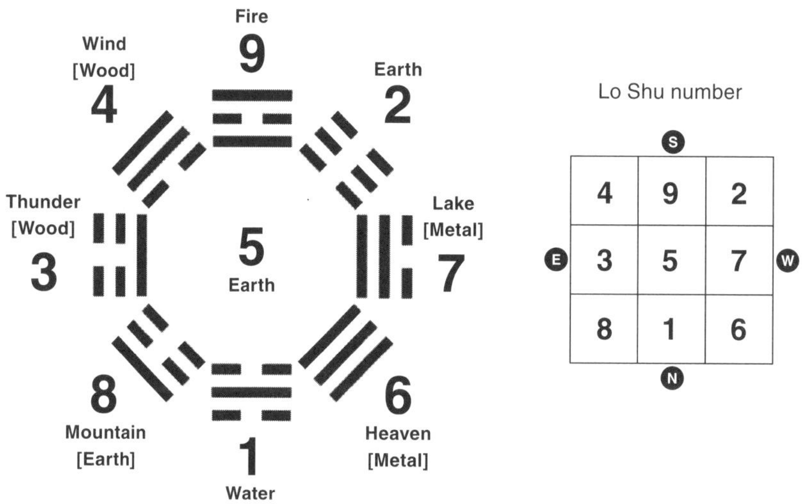

Figure 32: 8 Trigrams Later Arrangement and Lo Shu number

The Hoto Diagram

Another mysterious numerical diagram carried on the back of a "Fire Horse" and was discovered at the River Ho region around the same time.

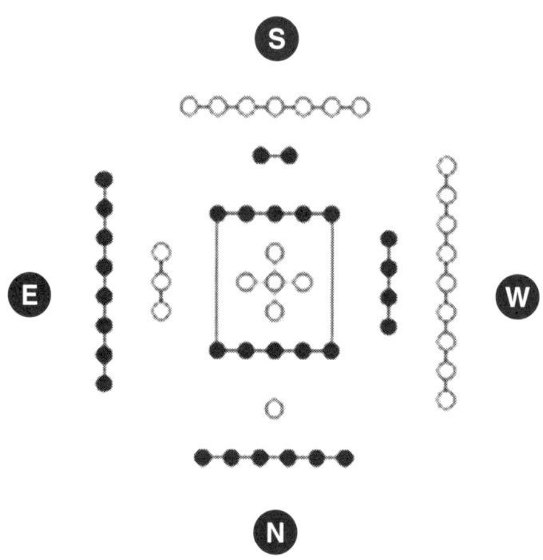

Figure 33: Hoto Diagram

Turning this figure of points into numbers results in the following.

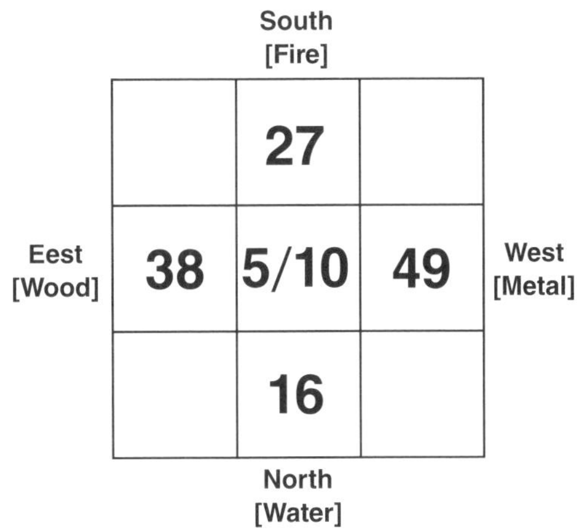

Figure 34: Hoto Numbers

How to Use Hoto Numbers

These pairs of numbers play a major role in combination in Flying Star feng shui appraisals. When these Hoto Combination Stars are present in adjacent bearings, if one of the numbers in the pair refers to an auspicious flying star, the other star also becomes auspicious.

Example

Figure 35: A Restaurant with an Age 7 East-Facing 2–3 Chart, Flying Star Chart

Since it is a commercial facility, we will only look at the Water Star (Wealth Star)

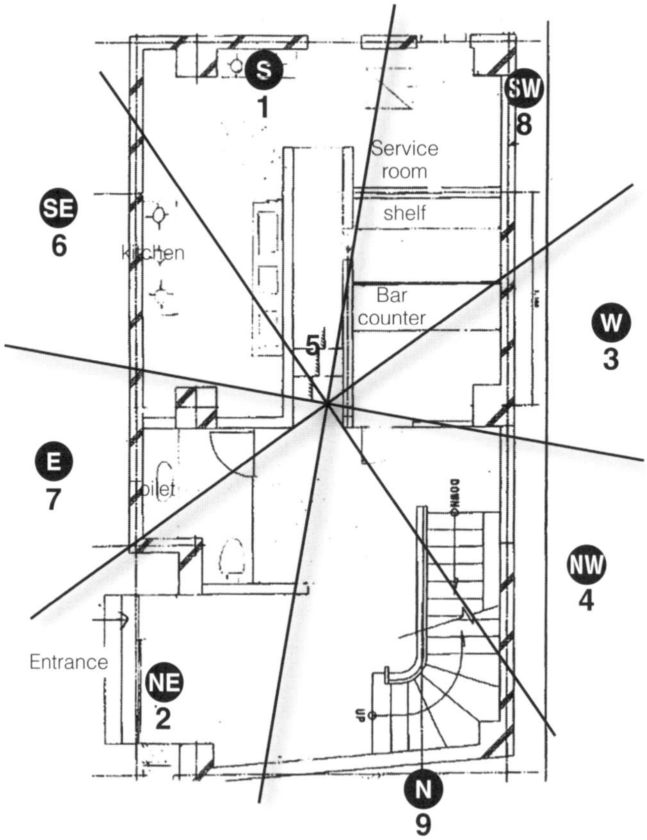

Figure 36: Floor Plan of the restaurant with the Wealth Stars

Age 7: If there is no wall between the East and Northeast bearing, there is a 2–7 Hoto Combination, meaning that Wealth Stars 2 and 7 will have the same energy and be very auspicious for economic fortune.

Age 8: If there is no wall between the West and Southwest bearing, there is a 3–8 Hoto Combination; activating this area will be very auspicious for economic fortune.

Age 9: Because there is a staircase in the North and Northwest bearing, there is no interruption in this area. It has a 4–9 Hoto Combination, which is very auspicious for economic fortune.

Age 1: If there is no wall between the South and Southeast bearing, the area has a 1–6 Hoto Combination; activating it will be very auspicious for economic fortune.

This building has seen a high turnover in its tenants.

The above floorplan shows the restaurant that was in the building in Age 8. The occupants split the Southwest and West bearings with a wall (making Hoto Combination 3–8 unusable), and the window for Wealth Star 8 in the Southwest was also blocked. After years of unprofitable business, the restaurant closed down.

These maps refer not only to Wealth Stars, but Spiritual Stars as well.

How to Create a Flying Star Chart

What follows is a description of how to create Flying Star charts for anyone who might be interested. If this is understood, it will be possible to create the charts for buildings constructed in Ages 6 to 9 that are found at the back of this book.

[NOTE]
As the Flying Star charts at the end of this book are included for the reader's convenience, they are all oriented with north as "up," but these instructions will set south as "up," following the traditional method.

1. Let's try to make a Flying Star chart for a building that faces southeast and was built in Age 1.

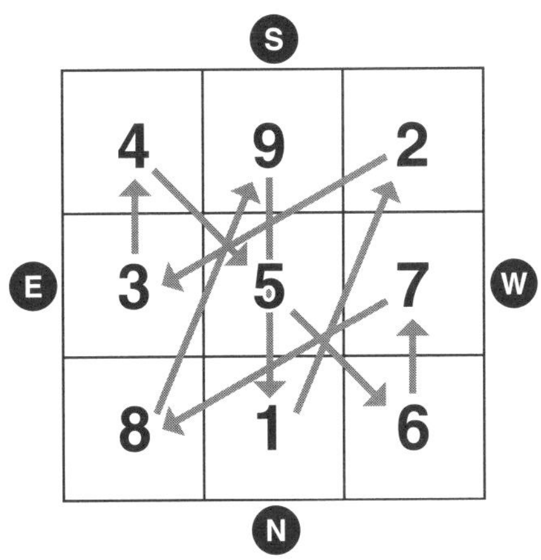

Figure 37: The direction that the numbers follow is always the same direction as Lo Shu.

2. Always put the number of the Age in the center bearing.

In this case, because it is an Age 1 building, place a 1 in the Center bearing, writing it in the same way as Lo Shu numbers proceed.

3. Write the number of the Facade Bearing (in this case, it is 7, for Southwest) to the upper right of the Age number in the Center bearing. Then, write the number of the opposite bearing (in this case 4, for Northeast) to the upper left of the Age number.

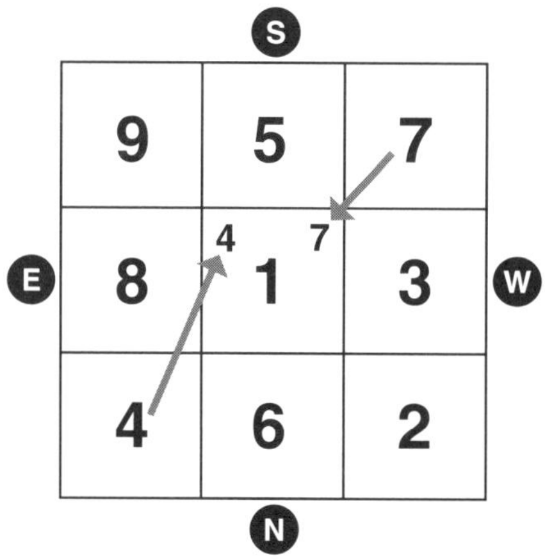

Figure 38: Period 1, Facing Direction SW1

The number on the right side is the Wealth Star, while the number on the right is the Spiritual Star.

Write down each number based on the following rules.

For Facing Direction 1 (example: SW1)

If the number of the Wealth or Spiritual Star in the middle is odd, go forward

If the number of the Wealth or Spiritual Star in the middle is even, go backwards

For Facing Direction 2–3 (example: SW2–3)

If the number of the Wealth or Spiritual Star in the middle is odd, go backwards

If the number of the Wealth or Spiritual Star in the middle is even, go forwards

Because the Facing Direction in this case, Southwest 1, is odd, go forwards from Wealth Star 7 (odd) and backwards from Spiritual Star 4 (even) in the Center.

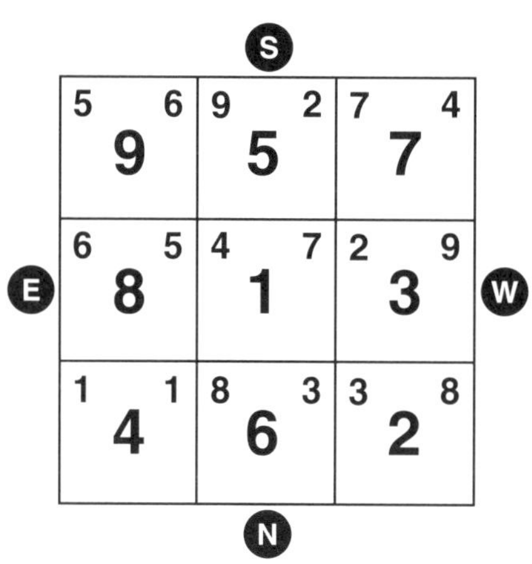

Figure 39: A Complete Flying Star Chart

The above is a Flying Star chart for an Age 1, Facing Southwest 1 building.

Exception

If the Spiritual and Wealth Star in the Center is 5, then treat the Star as odd if the number in the Center is odd, and even if it is even.

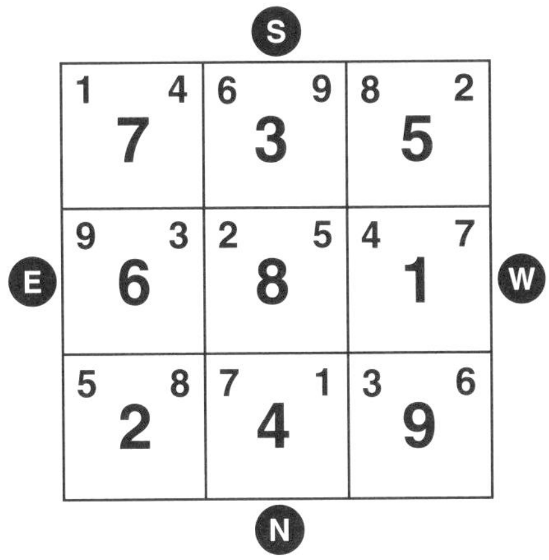

Figure 40: Example: Age 8, Facing Southwest 2–3 Chart

Because the Facing Direction is Southwest, the Wealth Star in the Center is 5. Because the Facade Bearing is 2–3, the rule is usually to go backwards if the number is odd; however, for Star 5 alone, it is treated as odd if the number in the middle is odd, and even if it is even. Here, the number in the middle is 8, so we go forwards.

Appendix

Appendix The flying star chart for age 6 (1964–1983)

S1

S2–3

SW1

SW2–3

W1

W2–3

NW1

NW2–3

Appendix The flying star chart for age 6 (1964–1983)

N1

N2–3

NE1

NE2–3

E1

E2–3

SE1

SE2–3

Appendix The flying star chart for age 7 (1984–2003)

S1

S2–3

SW1

SW2–3

W1

W2–3

NW1

NW2–3

Appendix The flying star chart for age 7 (1984–2003)

N1

N2–3

NE1

NE2–3

E1

E2–3

SE1

SE2–3

Appendix The flying star chart for age 8 (2004–2023)

S1

S2–3

SW1

SW2–3

W1

W2–3

NW1

NW2–3

Appendix The flying star chart for age 8 (2004–2023)

N1

N2–3

NE1

NE2–3

E1

E2–3

SE1

SE2–3

Appendix The flying star chart for age 9 (2024–2043)

S1

S2–3

SW1

SW2–3

W1

W2–3

NW1

NW2–3

Appendix The flying star chart for age 9 (2024–2043)

N1

N2–3

NE1

NE2–3

E1

E2–3

SE1

SE2–3

Appendix 2: The Direction Division Sheet

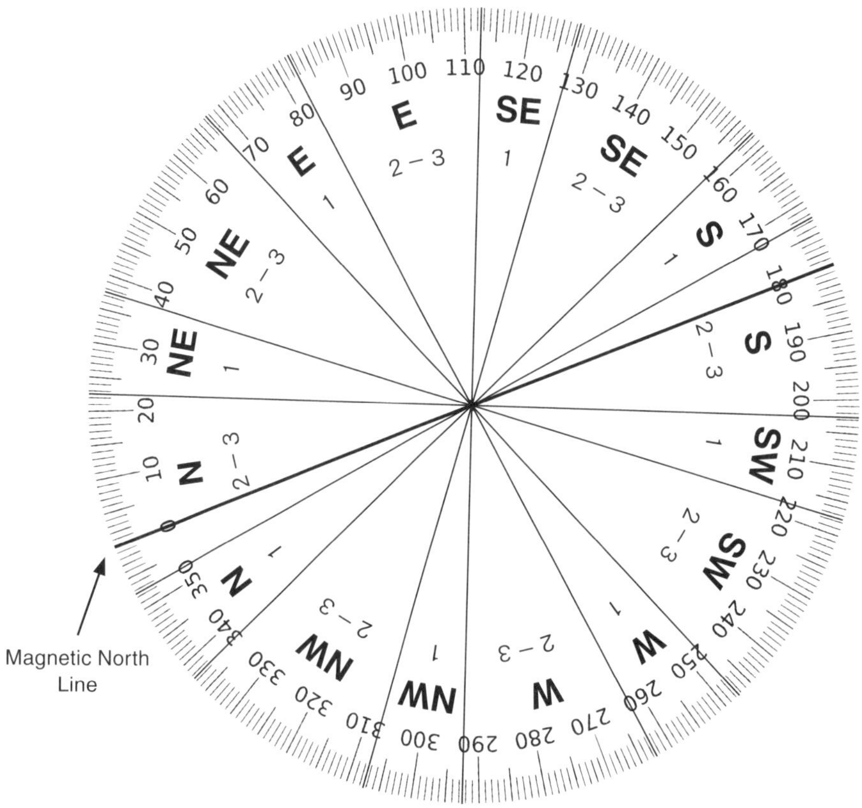

Afterword

Feng Shui is Not Magic

I happened to see an interview on Japanese TV with Audrey Tang, the Digital Minister of Taiwan, who contributed to the rapid COVID-19 response in her country. When asked at the end if she had anything to say to the Japanese people, her response, which she explained that she always said to everyone, was "Live long and prosper." At that point, without thinking, I fixed my eyes on her face.

Audrey Tang was reading classics by age 5, learning high school math by age 6, began self-study of programming at age 8, and started an IT company in Silicon Valley at 19. At 35, Tang withdrew from the business world and became the youngest cabinet minister in Taiwan in history. I remember feeling quietly moved that this accomplished person, who is also fluent in English and has revealed herself to be transgender, is carrying on the ideals of feng shui. To "live long and prosper" is precisely what feng shui seeks to achieve.

While Flying Star feng shui attempts to promote longevity and prosperity by manipulating the energy of indoor rooms, this includes not just personal prosperity, but the prosperity of one's descendants as well. It is said that a bedroom with an auspicious Spiritual Star will increase the chances of childbirth, but this cannot override one's existing destiny. Because it is difficult to prove that everyone will be satisfied, no attempts in this book have been made to claim so.

[*The whole of your earthly life is one long challenge and test. You are the center of a battlefield in which all the forces of your being wage constant war.*]

GUIDANCE FROM SILVER BIRCH
Edited by Anne Dooley
P.31 Chapter 4 Problem of suffering

If you try to use feng shui techniques in the hope that they are a kind of magic that can make dreams come true, liberate us from difficulty, or ensure we live our lives in this world just as we please, you will likely be disappointed.

China has a saying that the mandate of heaven is first, the destiny of man is second, and feng shui is third. In other words, there is no magical household that will allow one to completely escape their lot in life. The emperors of China never succeeded in attaining immortality, and every dynasty eventually met its end.

The charm of the techniques of Flying Star feng shui is in their precision, but this precision refers to the ability of a Flying Star chart to explain the broad strokes of the history of the tenants of a building. Even if a house is built according to feng shui to protect against any and all disasters, it is not possible to escape that which has been ordained by God, as candidly stated by someone who has used these techniques. Those difficulties that occur in spite of using feng shui techniques may be inescapable challenges that are necessary for spiritual growth.

The value of using feng shui lies in balancing the energy of one's living environment in order to maximize the natural financial, health, and relationship fortunes of its inhabitants. If, as Silver Birch says, this world is a battlefield for experimenting with the possibilities that our souls have hidden, then Flying Star feng shui offers a means for inspiring us to make that battlefield a little easier to live in.

The post-COVID-19 world may never go back to exactly how it was before. If we will now spend more time in our offices and homes, the importance of ensuring their environments is in order has only grown. If this book succeeds in introducing even a single person to these ancient, divine secrets, that will be enough for me.

Appendix 2: The Direction Division Sheet

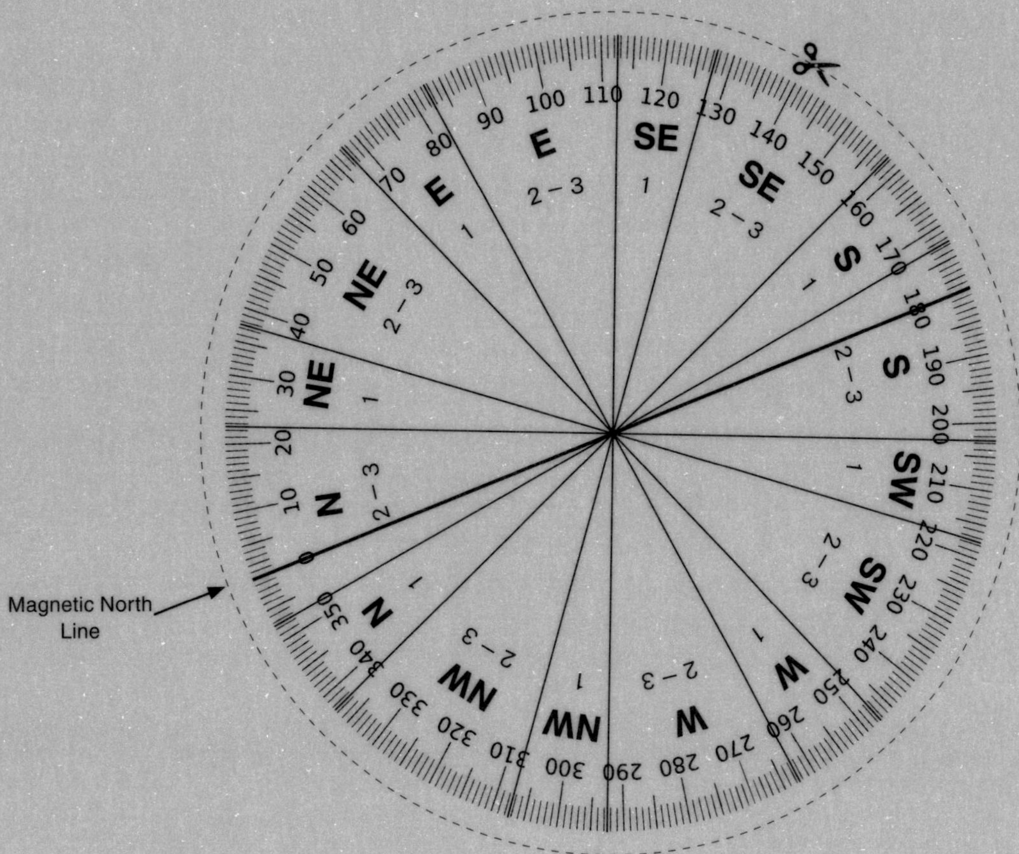

Appendix 2: The Direction Division Sheet

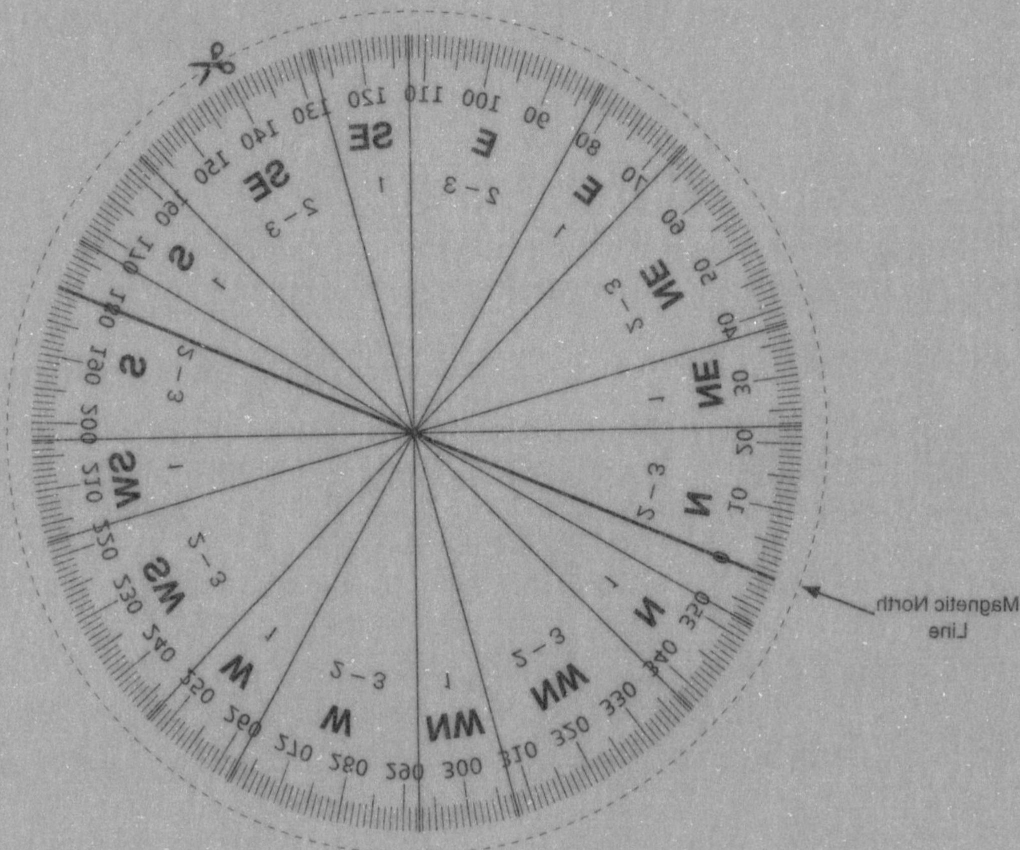